Writing Sensorably

OTHER TITLES BY M.A. PAYTON

Adventures of a Mainstream Metaphysical Mom:
Choosing Peace of Mind in a World of Diverse Ideas

"Soul"utions:
Achieving Financial, Intellectual, Physical, Social,
and Spiritual Balance with Soul

Birth Mix Patterns™:
Astrology, Numerology, and Birth Order, and their
Effects on the Past, Present, and Future

Birth Mix Patterns™:
Astrology, Numerology, and Birth Order, and their
Effects on the Families & Other Groups that Matter

Birth Mix Patterns™ and Loving Relationships
using Astrology, Numerology, and Birth Order

Healing What's Real:
Expanding Your Personal Power
with Mind Over Matter Techniques

Writing Sensorably

How Expressive and Natural Voice Advance Recording Thoughts

M. A. Payton
Author of
Adventures of a Mainstream Metaphysical Mom series,
Healing What's Real, *Birth Mix Patterns*™ series, and *"Soul"utions*

The Left Side
Asheville, North Carolina

Interior body text is set in 12 point Centar by Pete Masterson, Æonix Publishing Group, www.aeonix.com
Cover photo by L. Leigh Meriweather.

Copyright © 2014 **by Michelle Payton.** All rights reserved. No part of this book may be reproduced or copied in any form or by any means — graphic, electronic, or mechanical, including photocopying, taping, or information storage and retrieval systems — without written permission from the publisher.

ISBN 978-0-9719804-7-1 (paperback)
ISBN 978-0-9719804-8-8 (ePub)
LCCN: 2008902436

Published by
The Left Side
Asheville, North Carolina

www.theleftside.com

Printed in the United States of America

Contents

Acknowledgements 9
Introduction 11
    Sensory-Based Writing for Left
        and the Right Brainers 11
Sensory-Based Writing Framework 15
    Your Selfie Voice 15
    Gaining the Courage to Write 16
    Capturing the Natural Written Voice 18
    Silent Writing 20
    Where did Grammar and Punctuation Come From? 20
    Natural Pause Grammar and Sliding Scale
        Punctuation Polishing 22
    Setting Goals for Your Writing on Your Terms 25
    Putting your Custom Sensory-Based Writing Structure
        Together to Self-Facilitate 28
Easy-To-Follow Studies & Articles At-A-Glance 31
    No-Nonsense Studies, Academic Theories and
        Opinions on Writing in the Arts and Sciences 31
    The Damage that Comes with
        Not Accepting Ordinary Language 32
    Teens Write! To Hell with the System! 33
    Reading What You Connect With
        Is a Big Writing Deal 34

Standardize or Personalize? 35
Sciences Successfully Using Self-Reflection and
    Expressive Writing 36
Vibrant Writing using Hypnosis Techniques 37
Self-Hypnosis Increasing PhD Academic Output 37
Hypnosis and Imagery Improving Reading and
    Writing for the Everyday, Mindful Jane and Joe. 38
Enhanced Performance and Expressive Writing 39
Normal Speech in Writing: An Academic Perspective 39
Journaling with a Meditative Twist 41

Sensory-Based Tools In The Progressive Mainstream 43
What Type of Writer and Learner Are You?. 43
Self-Portrait Writing and
    Activating Sensory Experiences 46
Expanding Laboratory Work with
    Sensory-Based, Oral Storytelling. 49
Expressive Writing to Relieve Test Anxiety. 53

Sensory-Based Tools For Self-Help 59
Ordinary Writing to Soothe the Soul 59
Sensory-Based Writing and Beginning at the End. 60
Expressive Writing and Focusing on Adversity
    Opposites when Telling Your Story 63

Writers' Brainstorming Process 67
What to write about 67
What's the Problem? 68
Sensory-Based Detailed Problem Solving. 71

Writing On Passionate Subjects 75
Reading to Write and Speak. 75
Adversity as Building Blocks 76
Childhood Trauma 78
Prejudice. 79
Victim 83
Empowerment 86

Approaching Highly Charged Situations with Caution 88
Simple, Happy Memories 90
Reframing Perceptions 92
Change, the only Constant 95
Group Therapy Gone Bad................................... 97
Community 100
Joy of Family 104
Phobias... 106
Intimidation.. 108
The Intricacies of Being a Woman 110
Breaking Abusive Patterns................................ 113

Conclusion 117
    No excuses! Get to Writing!........................... 117

References 119

About The Author 123

Index 129

Acknowledgements

Thanks to all who granted permission to reference their good work so those who write in the arts, sciences, or simply for themselves have a deeper understanding of how their writing fits in the world.

Thank you to Dr. Diane Martinez, one of my professors in graduate school who gently prodded me to finish the MA program, and spent countless hours on my website and CV to help me understand how my background fits in academia, and the realities of when it doesn't. I appreciate Dr. Drew Virtue's flexible teaching style, who customized his graduate seminar to encourage students to publish within their chosen fields, and enabled this book to take shape (suggestions you and your students made were invaluable — with honorable mentions to graduate students Lauren Thomas and Joshua Bivens).

To Pete Masterson, my book designer, who agreed to continue to work with me even when officially retired. Your hand-holding has been invaluable over nearly fifteen years.

To my husband, Karl, who has been coerced to become a proofreader and patient listener (as I read aloud) of multiple thousands of pages of my writing over many decades. Thank you, also, for holding down a steady job so that I have the flexibility to take on projects like this book and many other ventures.

To my collaborators who have provided me space to facilitate, and students and clients who have attended my seminars and also served as my teachers.

Introduction

Sensory-Based Writing for Left and the Right Brainers

Writing *Sensorably* is for those who are interested in: ways to record as much content on paper as possible, as well as optimizing audio and video storytelling; improving performance through writing across numerous disciplines, as well as those who avoid disciplines; and softening the impact of past or upcoming stress. This is achieved by taking advantage of what you already have — your natural voice — and can range from self-help processing to scientific observations. Creative writing and journaling followers may (at first) gravitate to extending the writing experience using multiple senses — seeing, hearing, tasting, smelling, tactile or touching. The measurable-minded may find the referenced published papers and research demonstrating how natural voice and sensory-based writing contributes to even the most highly disciplined work most appealing. Ultimately, left and right-brained communicators and writers will understand how both connect and enhance storytelling, writing and even reading experiences.

In the least, discourse on the value of the natural voice and sensory-based experiences develop and encourage advancement in those interested (regardless of discipline) in recording thoughts on paper, audio, and even video. A conceptual framework in recording thoughts will be shared on a notion that has evolved over three decades as a result of my training as a mind over matter professional — Hypnosis, Neuro-linguistic programming and related solutions; a professional writer; and aspiring-but-on-my-own-terms academic addressing my challenges, as well as clients and students I have worked with. A number of studies, theories and opinions will be reviewed across disciplines. Natural voice concepts will then be put into practice with actual recording and writing samples that utilize framework steps to demonstrate how content is generated when one communicates about what one is most expert — reimaginable personal experiences (which include science skills). Ultimately, the importance of personal connection to material will be demonstrated and how that linking contributes to improvements on paper and other mediums.

The objective of this body of work is to record it on paper, but I'm as much a talker as a writer. Since this book is now in your hands, I will assume that you have an interest in pouring information from your head on to paper. The following assemblage of information and techniques carve out paths that you can eventually customize to your individual strengths to fully express your thoughts. I recommend, as you read, to keep a recording device — audio recorder, computer, or paper and pen — so that you can preserve your ideas.

Absorb each section. You may not agree with all of them as a result of past training or schooling, but give it a chance (I'll touch on that in the next paragraph). This is not a traditional banking approach with hard and fast rules (stuff information in the brain and see what sticks). While you would have major issues if this text weren't in a grammatically correct format at this moment, this is not a process that views grammar as the most important element to writing in the initial stages, as this slows the number of words initially generated during the recording process. In fact, punctuation in preliminary drafts is discouraged.

Taking a step back, to date everything you have learned and retained on how to get from writing point "a" to writing point "b" has value. While I can become frustrated with those who declare who are and are not real writers, you wouldn't be able to read this text without sticklers, rule mongers, and those who assign ranks to performance (I am, in fact, an enforcer of certain rules in academia as an English instructor). Eventually you will find that while we work with the natural voice and sensory realm to develop content in *Writing Sensorably*, we can revise and polish to play by others' rules as well. At the end of the day, however, you can't edit if there is nothing on paper.

Sensory-Based Writing Framework

Your Selfie Voice

Ten p.m. on a Saturday, my soon-to-be 13-year-old daughter has three girlfriends over for the night. Heads down in their cell phones and huddled together they snap selfies with intermittent "Look at this! Listen!" Or simply averting screens from their eyes to others in the group then giggling. Observing them around the kitchen table I hear, "Mrs. Bay" — *bay* is slang for being cool, but I create boundaries by insisting "Mrs." is added — "Look up!" A phone — now camera — zooms in on the contrasts that come from being a woman of age with one more youthful. An image is created, and with a quick finger flick is posted with a text caption. I am now a part of the autobiographical selfie archive for this young woman and hundreds of others are now witnesses. Young, expressive, recorders and writers are born.

Selfie, from my perspective, is an abbreviation for self-portrait that is, today, most often connected to digital recorders, phones and cameras. Classic artists throughout time have attached value to leaving paintings, drawings, photographs and sculptures of their likenesses to chisel out a place in history. Psychological examination aside on the attraction to the concept, the selfie (or self-portrait) is timeless, but now with a 21st century multi-modality twist accessible to millions of people from classic paintings to computer presentations, audio, video, and hardcopy and e-books.

Recording or writing a document that is eventually reviewable by you or others requires the ability to compose fluidly and involves a certain amount of knowledge on the subject, a bit of conviction, and maybe even a little passion. Self-reflection and autobiographies create immediate experts, but with study can be extended to other subjects. When confidence pours through your fingertips and your individual writing voice is established, content is abundant.

Gaining the Courage to Write

I'm not really sure how I developed the courage to write as my K-12 education was primarily spent in schools that served the lower income population where a 35 student class size was normal, many kids didn't complete assignments, and physical altercations and lethal weapons were common so teachers had to balance education with safety (their own as well as students).

I can recall, in eighth grade, when our class was assigned *David Copperfield* by Charles Dickens. I struggled through the 700+ page book on my own because I didn't want to seem like a know-it-all by asking questions — there were no in-class discussions or chapter goals. The week the class was supposed to finish the text the teacher asked, "Who started the book?" Some hands went up. "Who finished the book?" I was one of the few students whose hand remained in the air. She then announced, "We'll just cancel the assignment since, basically, no-one finished the book." My head said, "What!?" while my lips remained sealed. If I complained about the injustice I would be met after class by kids who would hold me responsible for their additional workload or bad grades.

More driven than soured by the experience, I continued to assume when work was assigned in school that I must complete it to the best of my abilities. My reward was good grades as I moved through school ranks. I had no clue if I was an effective writer. Essentially, no-one was watching, and ignorance was bliss (maybe even a bit delusional).

I went on to earn an undergraduate degree in Communication Arts, returned to academia in my 40's and 50's as graduate student in English, and over the past 30 years I have been a professional communicator: hired as a professional writer and strategist in corporations, successfully generated content as an independent writer, experimented qualitatively with students as an independent writing teacher, adjunct teach English and reading in college, and am a sensory trained professional in hypnosis and related mind over matter solutions. A personal concept evolved (as well as a structure) over three decades that: if one can think one can tell a story — in writing or orally; there are many ways to do this effectively; and (while some may believe they are) there is no absolute expert on the subject. The major challenge for me and those I have worked with to generate content — through visualization, speaking aloud, and putting words to paper — is self-confidence.

As a hypnosis and mind over matter solutions professional, my role is to co-facilitate generating content through imagery and, when appropriate, speaking and writing. Information is gathered by accessing memories, and to walk clients deeper into recall we gather sensory data: see, hear, touch, smell, and taste. I use a similar process to effectively lengthen work on paper, with certain elements initially adhered to so that the natural written voice is heard (prior to the polish stage):

- writing about something known (from autobiographical to highly studied including science),
- in first person,
- focusing on the present tense,
- no punctuation,
- no editing while writing (crossing information out is acceptable so text is not completely lost),
- no erasers, and
- structured introductory paragraphs are discouraged (not to be confused with not being focused as we must have some subject to broach).

CAPTURING THE NATURAL WRITTEN VOICE

When I was in elementary school my Grandfather became my pen pal (no computers, written by hand, requiring an envelope and stamp). Brainstorming on coming up with a few lines for Grandpa evolved to love letters to boyfriends, holiday newsletters to former neighbors and business colleagues, and letters to friends who moved to other cities. I recall writing a letter to an acquaintance and she responded, "You write the same way you talk. I could actually hear your voice when I read your letter." "Was that good," I wondered? Since I loved to talk I chose, "Yes."

As I wrote professionally for a company magazine and newsletter, I allowed myself to write as I spoke and I noticed I generated a lot more content as a result. My manager didn't always like my style — I worked for a manufacturing company that was accustomed to a more impersonal approach — but management above her found it refreshing so some of my key pieces made the corporate cut. My confidence was building.

When I wrote my first book — *Adventures of a Mainstream Metaphysical Mom* — feedback included, "I can hear your voice." This time I knew, "Yes, that's a good thing, I'm reaching others." And when I decided that I was interested in teaching others how to develop content, I taught what I knew, of course — the natural voice is easier to write and interesting to read.

When developing natural written voice writing, one exercise I do with students is to capture a story shared out loud with a recording device and I then ask questions. For instance, the student might reminisce, "I was walking on the beach." I would interrupt, "Be there, in the moment, in present tense. What is the weather like? What color is the sand? What are you wearing? How are you interacting with the sand? What do you hear? What do you smell? When you smell sometimes you get a taste sensation, what is that like? How are your legs and feet resisting when walking on the beach?" All of these questions would be answered and if the student responds, "I don't know" (similar to writer's block), my reply would be something like "Let's build a bridge and get close to what it can be, realistically."

Each student talks through (as if in the present) what is likely to be an accurate picture of an experience and then transcribes her natural voice on paper (deleting my verbal prompts to hear only her story) — What am I experiencing? What am I seeing, smelling, tasting, hearing, feeling on my skin...? Confidence builds as the writing utensil remains in motion — a pattern reprogramming technique that creates new muscle memory, when executed consistently the brain shape actually changes configuration. Once adopting a new pattern or thinking process over a three-week period, the motion becomes natural. It's important to note that initially punctuation is represented with a symbol like an "x," star, smiley face, heart or other nonsensical symbol where the writer senses natural pauses (because grammar usage is more linear, it takes the brain out of creative mode — is a content deflating process — and is reviewed later in the process).

Silent Writing

The next exercise is rewriting the same story without looking at what was transcribed which is labeled silent writing (I have taken an eraser from a writer's hand during this stage). While I have had strong audio learners in seminars that can recount their original stories nearly verbatim, most come up with additional material. Once work is on paper, each student reads the natural written voice and silent writing. During author readings, each is asked to notice natural breathing and pausing while speaking and can mark papers with the symbol.

The group then discusses the process (this can also be done one-on-one), each body of work, and then moves into the polish stage. To generate optimal content, when moving into polish stage, the natural voice transcription and silent writing exercises are combined (removing repetitive text). When experiencing writer's block or simply expanding a piece, processes to consider include:

- silent writing then repeating aloud;
- orally storysharing, recording, transcribing, then silent writing;
- silent writing, reading aloud and expanding the story aloud while recording.

You will come up with your optimal mix, but the eerie part is (when doing this enough) you begin to hear voices in your head. Luckily, at least in many cases, it's your own!

Where did Grammar and Punctuation Come From?

In order to come up with a process, one must be able to connect the dots, and associate one piece of information with another. I became frustrated with any system that assumed my brain was merely a bank — insisting that depositing information through memorization was the answer.

Memorization is done in chunks, regurgitated during exams, and then lost if there is no real world association. So to make sense of why grammar and punctuation were approached in certain ways, I wondered where the practice originated.

Writing utensils and surfaces were difficult to come by in the early days of Greek writing so it was common to see a page of textwithoutanyspacesor punctuationtorecordasmanywordsaspossibleonasurface. There are a number of opinions on where punctuation originated. Some say it was the result of Irish monks attempting to make translations of sacred text more clear, others say it is a result of actors adding marks to scripts to express themselves more naturally on stage (much like what is seen on sheet music). There is likely some truth to both of these stories, and what they have in common is an interest in making things easier — adding white space and pauses make artful, common sense. The good news is, today there are ways to make the grammar and punctuation process more intuitive.

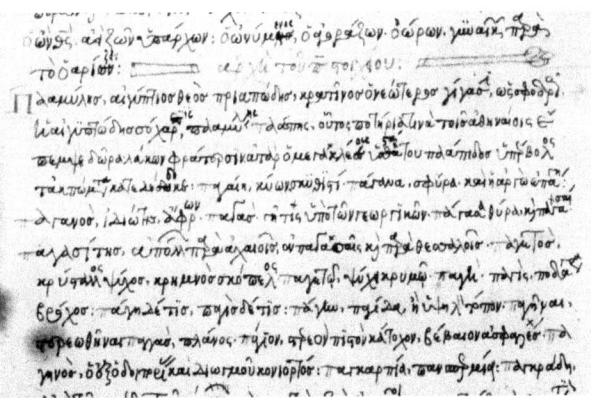

Sample of Greek Writing

Natural Pause Grammar and Sliding Scale Punctuation Polishing

Polishing with punctuation marks is only permitted following content building with oral sharing, transcribing natural written voice and the silent writing. (I will confess, there are times when writers slip in a period or comma here or there, but most of the time symbols are used instead of punctuation.) Forms of — and insecurities that might come with — Standard Written English will re-enter the process; however, a writer has a new awareness and habits to add to the writing mix to encourage advancement. Advanced punctuation is one of my weaknesses, and Dawkins' "meaning-based punctuation" (2003) had a profound impact on me in my first year of graduate school. Academic clouds literally parted when I read that grammar and punctuation usage could be put into a more personal context and it would be considered correct. No memorization! Finally, I didn't have to push back! Well, at least, some of the time.

Imagine my excitement when I also found academics arguing (in certain scenarios) to put natural voice back into the writing process. While punctuation and grammar can be an intimidating part of the process, I and writers that I've worked with have come to understand that they have more individual, decision-making power when using what I term "sliding value punctuation" and "natural pause grammar."

To keep the writing momentum and self-confidence intact during the revision and polish stage — adding even more freeing, personalized steps to Dawkin's grammar concept (more on Dawkin's work in the research section) — a student can build an individual grammar chart. Marks could equal a few to up to a dozen: comma, dash, parenthesis, colon, semicolon, period, exclamation point, question mark, ellipses points, no mark. Each writer ranks in a way that makes sense to her (see fig. 1).

Rank (most to least often)	Mark	Comments
Final Point	. (period)	Final mark. End of thought or discussion.
Separating, Interrupting, Listing, and Pausing Point	, (comma)	Many times used to separate and, but, for, so, or, nor, yet. Used in a sentence to interrupt a thought, introduce a subject within the same sentence, or create a natural pause when reading aloud.
Changing-a-thought Point	— (dash)	When changing tone, adding, or interrupting a thought in the same sentence, dashes create more of an emphasis than parenthesis or commas.
Defining or Listing Point	: (colon)	When introducing a word, phrase, or concept: then providing more details or a listing of items.
As a side-note and somewhat still on the subject Point	( ) (parenthesis)	When a subject should be mentioned in the text at that time, but more of a sidenote.
No mark		Just because there is a pause when reading aloud, doesn't always mean one should punctuate. Commas and periods are the safest, and most often used marks in many works.
Extending a thought Point	; (semicolon)	Easy to use incorrectly, and not a great mark for those who don't like taking punctuation chances. A semicolon is commonly used when extending an explanation on a subject.

Figure 1. Example of Sliding Scale Punctuation

For example, one may constantly interrupt her thoughts when speaking so parenthesis and dashes may be higher ranking marks on her scale than one who finishes a succinct thought, then moves onto the next. Note that you don't have to agree with the figure provided. That's the point. You're the boss! The sliding scale punctuation chart could also be standardized for those who believe there is a pure approach as well (applied to teaching groups, for instance). A great way to decide what grammar and punctuation you are most comfortable with is by emulating how you see it done in your favorite reading material — ranging from technical manuals on how to fix something, magazines, and the most highly acclaimed literary work. Habitual writers should consider keeping personal sliding scale punctuation chart diaries next to your bed stands or in your pockets and change it when it suits your fancy. More relaxed writers will, likely, keep it very simple, just notice usage here and there, and make a mental note.

Process-wise, to understand what type of punctuating writer and storyteller you are at this moment (and it does change), begin logging what punctuation makes sense to you in all reading material. The premise — as in hypnosis and related mind over matter solutions, Gee's (2007) book and other studies referenced in the research section — is that when reading you relate to the usage, you see it in action. Don't just attach this to classic literature. Apply this also to fun reads, and the *un*classics. Every now and again — with more challenging punctuation marks in particular — I will write "; usage," for instance, in the margin (the semicolon is one of my challenge marks). When I feel comfortable with marks I have been known to overuse them, according to my editors (I'll get comments like, "What's up with all the '—' usage?"), but at the end of the written day periods and commas are used most often. Master those and expanded usage will make more sense when you want to change voice. But, your very own voice matters in this process.

From a natural pause grammar perspective, Peter Elbow (his work will be addressed in more detail in the research section) shares ways to harmoniously combine the idea of rhetorical punctuation — following voice pauses and speaking intonations that emphasize intended meaning that is also used to clarify text in the theatre and seen on sheet music — with grammar rules that are commonly accepted. Ultimately, this creates punctuation that's good enough and is perceived as literate. (When attempting to impress with advanced punctuation it doesn't always work out so why go there?) An important note is Peter Elbow emphasizes in *Vernacular Eloquence* that this doesn't mean a punctuation mark will end in every oral pause, nor does it mean that every mark will be correct to every viewer (rules still apply with style sheets from publications or academic requirements, and personal opinions can count at times).

There are countless books on styles, how to punctuate and use grammar. With sensory-based and self-portrait type writing, and personalized grammar and punctuation; however, certain steps are intentionally not covered in this text as the focus is *increasing* content. This concept is about self-standardization that can complement other regulated output when in polish stages.

Setting Goals for Your Writing on Your Terms

A teacher on my Facebook newsfeed posted, "I like rubrics. There, I said it. They make my grading life easier."

First, allow me to explain that an academic rubric is something that teachers and academic institutions use to standardize grading systems. From administrators' points of view, they can establish what is most important for a project and apply to all students to manage expectations, and keep grading fair and linear (even though grading is truly subjective). Maybe you can recall K-12 or college or if your children (if you are a parent) came home with a table showing items like figure 2.

	Exemplary (4 Points)	Proficient (3 Points)	Satisfactory (2 Points)	Unsatisfactory (1 Point)
Content - Main Idea Clear - Sound Research				
Organization - Introduction - Closing - Transitions - Logical Development				
Language Use - Grammar - Punctuation - Style - Vocabulary				
Delivery & Voice - Volume - Clarity - Intonation - Pace - Gestures				

Figure 2. Academic Rubric.

Being a bit of a nonconformist, I have a difficult time with standardization, so when I was required as a graduate student to use a rubric for a research project I was offended. "Really? At this level in academia?" I admit I grumbled to the professor about this, but then I experienced an aha moment as the standardized format evolved to a brilliant idea — the exercise was to create a rubric unique to each student's work. We created individual rubrics and turned them in with our work so that the professor could assign grades from the goals we set for our work. Reframing the idea, it became a rubric collaboration (for students less committed to writing, there could be a group discussion that could be translated to more of a rubric democracy — what all students should focus on for a class project).

The rubric conversation sparked an idea for sensory-based writing, of course, when moving into polish stage. It's an ever-changing, customized rubric where you may be focusing on strengthening weaknesses as well as keeping yourself on track (figure 3).

Clear & Engaging Thesis Statement	Not too dry. Purpose is clear, but conversational.
Insightful Research	Evidence is engaging and on topic. Research isn't dry and makes sense to targeted readers.
Effective Voice Management	Combines and transitions research and creative aspects effectively.
Clear Organization and Flow	Introduction captures the reader. Transitions from section to section flow.

Figure 3. Ever-changing, customized rubric

Standard rubrics have a place in certain situations. As much as I gripe, I have to adhere to some standardization when teaching in college. But, where possible, add self-standardization on your personal writing "to do" list (like holding your own feet to the fire) to become a more effective communicator.

Putting your Custom Sensory-Based Writing Structure Together to Self-Facilitate

To help you add structure to your independent practice, the following is a basic outline of how I work one-on-one or one-on-many (manageable-sized workshops). Note that this changes depending on writer needs, but it gets you started.

Writing Outline:

1. Review *Learning Styles Assessment for Audio, Visual, Tactile*.
2. Prep your recorder then oral storyshare (self-facilitate by heightening sensory-based experiences — see, taste, smell, touch);
3. Transcribe your natural written voice (no punctuation — okay, maybe random periods and commas that don't stop your flow — use your symbol only).
4. Break as needed.
5. Silent write, expand twists & turns, you can cross out (no erasing or deleting);
6. Read aloud (both natural written voice and silent writing to compare voices);
7. Break from your writing and notice your natural style, then create your customized sliding scale punctuation table.
8. Create your customized rubric to decide what your priorities are for your writing project.
9. Return to the sensory-based writing process.
10. When polishing combine natural written voice (transcribed), Silent writing, and ordinary voices in your head writing (not transcribed, natural voice).

11. Refer to the sliding scale punctuation, and customized rubric for consistency and standardization on your terms.
12. Customize the process to your learning style and liking, once you get a feel for the flow.

Expanding a bit on the outline, details on learning styles can be found in the *What Type of Writer and Learner Are You?* section. In the provided outline, I have assumed that you have a writing project in mind so moving onto oral storysharing, consider saying aloud in ordinary language (and audio record):

- what you're writing about (a summary that could also contribute to an outline of topics);
- some like outlines, but begin your writing where you have a lot to say (not necessarily at the beginning, you'll edit this later);
- your professional or personal vision;
- how you would like your readers to view your work;
- your personal story or biography (if your goal is to publish).

Notice your language and natural pause style once you've made it through at least one complete cycle of oral storysharing, transcribing, silent writing, and reading aloud (to yourself or others). Put to paper what your personalized sliding value punctuation chart looks like, then create your customized rubric found in the *Setting Goals for Your Writing on Your Terms* section to serve as a focus tool.

During the polish stage you will combine elements of your natural and silent written work, including non-transcribed thoughts (ordinary voice in your head), utilize your punctuation and rubric tables, and revise to a more formal voice and style sheet if needed. Edit a paragraph or two here and there to prove that the process works for you (I would expect you to tweak the system here and there to fit your specific needs). However, put editing thoughts and tables out of your mind and return to sensory-based writing until word count is to your liking and your message is fully expressed.

Easy-To-Follow Studies & Articles At-A-Glance

No-Nonsense Studies, Academic Theories and Opinions on Writing in the Arts and Sciences

Storytelling — aloud and on paper — is a communication skill that comes in many shapes. Stories can be technical, artistic, healing or a combination of two or more, but all result in advancement. The following published work has been pieced together to demonstrate how sensory-based, self-portrait and personally relatable writing and storytelling — on paper and aloud — contribute to content generation to meet various ends which includes academic theories and opinions in the arts and sciences:

- how and why college students feel insecure about their writing abilities (Holland, 2013),
- findings on teens' interests in writing (Lenhart, Arafeh, Smith, & Macgill, 2008),
- how science exploration is boosted through freewriting or journaling (Balgopal, Meena, & Wallace, 2013),
- how expressive writing raises scores in students preparing for high stakes exams (Frattaroli, Thomas, & Lyumbomirsky, 2011),

- how hypnotherapy creates more writing content (Schultz, 1977 and Marinelli, 2012),
- how reading and writing are positively impacted by hypnosis, self-hypnosis, and related processes in imagery (Bhullar, Schutte & Malouff, 2011; Moffet, 1983; Fillmer & Parkay, 1985; and Stanton, 1986),
- how to reframe grammar and punctuation to match your ordinary voice (Dawkins, 2003 and Elbow, 2012),
- reading and writing silently and aloud to provide more individualized meaning to writers (Elbow, 2012; Frey, 1980; Gee, 2007; and Perin et al., 2003) and,
- authentic voice writing taught at universities for better writing and therapeutic environments for spiritual and emotional health (Metcalf & Simon, 2002).

The Damage that Comes with Not Accepting Ordinary Language

Peer reviewed, academic writing serves a purpose among the educated, but is a small, elite body of work that doesn't necessarily connect to a larger population interested in finding voice outside of academic or scholarly formatted boundaries. Bodies of work using natural or ordinary voice have been rejected by those who have more rigid standardized English rules which squelch confidence in would-be-writers. For instance, a community college case study focuses on students of African descent (American and other countries) and their dialect challenges, writing anxieties and situations in life. Most of these students were interested in writing — one case study revealed a poet who proudly shared her work in familial circles, but not in academia. Students' work in this study were labeled as substandard in academia due to the lack of acceptance of what is considered ordinary language (including one student's writing assessed as "ghetto" by a teacher), which resulted in decreased confidence when writing (Holland, 2013). Honoring the natural voice — aloud and on paper — is one step toward building confidence, or academic blinders will be ignored by certain populations' altogether.

TEENS WRITE! TO HELL WITH THE SYSTEM!

Pew Research (Lenhart et al., 2008) showed that when 1354 teens were asked what type of writing they preferred, the number one response (see

Enjoyment of Different Types of Writing % of teens who enjoy their...		
	School writing (n=697)	Non-school Writing (n=657)
A great deal	17%	49%
Some	50	41
Not much	22	8
Not at all	10	2

Source: Pew Internet & American Life Project Teen/Parent Survey on Writing, September-November 2007. Margin of error is ±5%.

Figure 4. Enjoyment of Different Types of Writing

fig. 4) showed 49% enjoyed "non-school writing . . . a great deal" (only 17% preferred school writing "a great deal"). Those who enjoyed non-school writing "a great deal" wrote notes to people (72%), preferred journaling (57%), and short (52%) and creative (45%) writing (see fig. 5). It's clear that these teens are going to write regardless of academic acceptance or rules. Providing reading and writing tools that are customized to match their expressions — as they journal, and pen short and creative work — advance their confidence and efforts (perhaps, over time, increasing interest in school and more formal writing). But, when opting out of academic

Non-school Writing Enjoyment and Activities % of teens who have done the following writing activities outside of school in the past year...		
	Enjoy non-school writing a great deal (n=331)	Enjoy non-school writing some or not much (n=313)
Write notes or letters to other people	72%	66%
Write in a journal	57*	16
Do short writing	52*	16
Do creative writing	45*	9
Write music or lyrics	38*	14
Create presentations	21*	13
Write essays	12*	4
Write computer programs	7	6

Source: Pew Internet & American Life Project Teen/Parent Survey on Writing, September-November 2007. Margin of error is ±5%. * indicates statistically significant difference between the percentages in the row.

Figure 5. Non-School Writing Activities.

writing is not possible, self-assurance plummets and anxiety rises. In an attempt to calm university students, research has gone as far as proving that breathwork, meditation, and guided imagery *before* beginning an essay or paper helps reduce apprehension (Martinez, Kock, & Cass, 2011).

Reading What You Connect With Is a Big Writing Deal

Reading is another solution to enhance overall writing comfort and competence, including for pleasure. A Columbia University study addresses reading and writing connections by studying 209 students in 13 community colleges. Ultimately, the finding was if one reads well then one writes well which also emphasizes the importance of being able to relate personally to text (Perin et al., 2003). When text is more challenging and less engaging, this can be overcome by using imagery or accessing sensory techniques (see, hear, taste, smell, and touch) so readers are more relaxed during the interpretation process. Frey's (1980) study focuses on the importance of relaxation to enhance reading performance of disabled readers in grades four through six. Students were coached in imagery (a form of self-hypnosis, creating a story — real or imagined — in the mind's eye) for 15 minutes per week and were asked to independently practice two to three times per day for a couple of minutes. The findings are that reading and writing performance are raised significantly compared to the control group (those who didn't practice imagery).

STANDARDIZE OR PERSONALIZE?

Returning to the idea of personally connecting to text, Gee (2007) argues in *What Video Games Have To Teach Us About Learning and Literacy* that human learning is based on past memories to make sense of the world and new experiences. Therefore, giving children abstract concepts to memorize without arranging information into some type of personal context sets children up to fail. Children have created their own framework when playing intricate video games — read and write extensive text, design games, research how to improve performance, and problem solve — and are similar skills that teachers seek in the classroom. Using an example of a seminar Gee offered, he asked teachers to read a video game manual that is easily referenced, for pleasure, by young people. Teachers quickly became frustrated because they couldn't comprehend the information. Gee's follow-up point is this is how kids feel when reading something in science without personal reference points. So the goal is for academic work to be relatable, resulting in a similar commitment found with video gamers willing to: explore unfamiliar ground, perform to become competent, and acquire new language and vocabulary to reach various goals.

From a rhetorical perspective, text is simply coding that makes sense once read and put into a context to enable understanding — this varies by cultures, genders, age, and backgrounds. One of the reasons why contemporary tools — like video games — are so enticing is the need of the individual is fulfilled (entertaining, reaching goals, feeling of accomplishment). According to Gee (2003), the more successful digital games are challenging yet attainable because players are permitted to customize games to their learning capabilities and sensory styles (i.e. audio, visual, or tactile). Increasing motivation further, gamers have the capability to self-test prior to playing, then adjust and co-create options to match their distinct skill sets. Overall, video gamers are left with a sense of self-empowerment.

Sciences Successfully Using Self-Reflection and Expressive Writing

More than fun and games, multiple disciplines have benefited when considering first person writing and individual voice. The National Association of Biology Teachers reported that science literacy increased across the board from middle school to college undergraduates when journaling in the moment to capture subtle nuances of experiments then retelling the experience in less formal settings (in addition to lab reports). Results included both science exploration and in-class discussions being boosted (Balgopal, Meena, & Wallace, 2013).

Expressive, in the moment, writing has also increased scores for graduate students preparing for MCAT (medical school entrance exam) and LSAT (law school entrance exam). Participants' baselines were taken on signs of depression, thoughts that distracted students from their exams, and cognitive or mental anguish that accompanied anxiety related to testing. Eighty-eight percent of the study group were taking high stakes entrance exams for the first time. The group that was asked to express deep thoughts and feelings about their exams on paper (nine days prior to the actual experience) showed significantly higher marks (in addition to showing less depression and anxiety) than the neutral group that didn't write about the upcoming experience (Frattaroli, Thomas, & Lyumbomirsky, 2011).

Vibrant Writing using Hypnosis Techniques

A program called "The Story Workshop" (Schultz, 1977) focuses on sharing thoughts aloud as well as on paper. Facilitators advise students to see (in the mind's eye) or recall exact or imagined scenes, guide students through the process with oral exercises, read aloud, write in the third person and in the present (Schultz, 1977) to increase output. Trained coaches walk students through hearing, smelling, feeling, and observing — much like hypnotherapists guide clients through imagery — to put voices to paper. Thirty years later, academics explored hypnosis in a multiple university study to test the performance of 320 hypnotizable subjects and found writing to be more vibrant and inventive in various writing categories: larger numbers of metaphors, similes, and abstract nouns, for instance (Marinelli, 2012).

Self-Hypnosis Increasing PhD Academic Output

Hypnosis or trance-like states aren't mysterious, but natural states that you experience everyday; for instance, when mindlessly showering or brushing your teeth, walking, driving, drinking tea or coffee and something pops into your mind out of (what seems to be) nowhere. You are accessing information from your subconscious mind. To clarify, hypnosis and self-hypnosis are the same type of relaxed state. Hypnosis usually includes a professional facilitator trained in techniques to aid an individual to achieve certain types of visualization. Self-hypnosis is when the individual achieves similar types of visualization alone.

Harry Stanton (1986) studied 27 academics dealing with writer's block that used a number of hypnosis or self-hypnosis techniques to improve output. He shared individual examples of one PhD who produced only three articles in seven years, and after using hypnosis techniques he produced 22 manuscripts in three years with 17 being published. Another academic hadn't published in 20 years then self-hypnosis (following scripts on her own) increased her output to 17 published articles in four years.

Stanton admits that this process doesn't work for everyone; however, the odds are high with 21 of the 27 (77%) improving output significantly.

Hypnosis and Imagery Improving Reading and Writing for the Everyday, Mindful Jane and Joe

An earlier mentioned study showed that reading improves writing (Perin et al., 2003), and adding imagery exercises to the equation improves reading (Frey, 1980). Fillmer and Parkay (1985) suggest specific scripts to use in the classroom that include imagery with the goal to motivate students to read, but formats would vary depending on the class age, personalities, interests, and experiences as well as teachers' comfort zones. In addition, Moffet (1983) points out that children between ages eight and twelve are highly receptive to text, and proposes that this prepuberty age group is also very open to suggestion in hypnosis. The concept is ego and peer pressure are not as much of an obstacle and readers are more willing to imagine scenes in the mind's eye. For all ages, identifying with material (subject, characters, and messages) is paramount so that information can be individually integrated resulting in inner growth and higher consciousness.

Writing is an additional extension to consciousness. The action transports the mind elsewhere — like reading — but once on paper the recall and imagery flesh out aha moments, gets stories straight in writers' heads, and connects to readers. Moffet (1983) takes reading and writing one step further, linking them to meditation saying that all three are deliberate acts to jump inside one's mind, create altered states of consciousness, and transformation.

Enhanced Performance and Expressive Writing

In a study covered earlier, expressive writing created an altered consciousness for graduate students taking high-stakes exams (Frattaroli, Thomas, & Lyumbomirsky, 2011). Expressive writing was also explored in connection with positive experiences of 46 individuals: meaningful, highly enjoyable, and reflections on how satisfaction from those activities can continuously fuel optimism. This type of writing resulted in higher levels of well-being psychologically and socially including less depression, anxiety, and stress when compared the group of 44 who wrote about simple regular activities (Bhullar, Schutte & Malouff, 2011). Taking this even one emotional step further, research with 86 dating couples who wrote expressively about their relationships showed they were more likely (than those who simply wrote about daily activities) to be dating three months later (Slatcher & Pennebaker, 2006). With expressive writing comes one's ordinary voice, and there is a 21st century movement to use normal speech in academic documents as well.

Normal Speech in Writing: An Academic Perspective

Peter Elbow's book *Vernacular Eloquence* shares what speech can bring to the table and his interest in gaining acceptance of hearing ordinary voice in academic writing. Elbow points to highly respected writers who have used normal speaking to advance their work like: Charles Darwin; Anne Frank (the *Diary of Anne Frank*); Nobel Prize winner, Richard Feynman, who produced major bodies of work through dictation; and Bertrand Russell. In the days of old, natural voice ruled in top corporations — executive secretaries were trained in shorthand (abbreviated symbols that increase the speed of writing versus spelling out all words and phrases) so that they could quickly and accurately jot down a memo that the boss would dictate aloud. She would then type — spell, punctuate and grammatically correct, maintain natural or formalize voice — the memo for his review and signature.

Elbow argues that no written language is pure — including grammar. Beginning to write without worrying about standard practices means writing projects actually start. Adding punctuation to the equation, confidence can be further deflated and can keep a project from being finalized. To reframe this process, he shows many examples of (what are perceived as) great writers taking creative license with punctuation that he labels rhetorical usage, and also references the work of John Dawkins as another possible solution to gaining self-assurance.

Moving out of the content generating stage and into polishing or standardizing — a contributor to apprehension when finalizing work — Dawkins (2003) shared a process on thoughtful punctuation that creates more individual meaning when polishing a piece of work. He achieved this through creating a hierarchy that ranks marks from zero to six – zero meaning no punctuation, to usage of a comma, dash, colon, semicolon, and period. Combining reading aloud, supplementing with reading, listening, and hearing meaning — along with a solid knowing of how and why five basic marks are ranked — writers of all levels and disciplines create optimal final drafts.

Journaling with a Meditative Twist

Taking fixed measurement completely out of the equation, there is another style of writing that is taught at universities to enhance writing and therapeutic environments for spiritual and emotional health called the proprioceptive method. The objective is not to go into polish stage (this writing is not intended for a reading audience), and to free yourself from performance judgment.

You continuously write in solitude for twenty-five minutes, on white unlined paper (lines are removed from the process to take the school atmosphere out of the process), light candles when you begin and blow them out at the end (an anchor to indicate you are beginning and ending a type of meditative ritual), burn incense, listen to slow and calming baroque music that plays for the full amount of writing time, with no drinks or snacks to disrupt the writing flow.

With this process you silent write using the voice you hear in your head. Writing content is expanded by asking a mantra question, "What do I mean by _____ ?" Academics, educators, professional writers, and those who have no interest in publishing at all have found this process to be ground breaking.

Sensory-Based Tools In The Progressive Mainstream

What Type of Writer and Learner Are You?

When I have worked with groups interested in or deciding that they no longer want to hate writing, one of the more appreciated pieces of information they walk away with is what type of writer they are. More accurately stated is, what is their most prominent learning style: visual, audio or tactile? Of course many have eyes, ears, and a sense of touch, but there is usually a number one preference, then two and three. As a trained professional in hypnosis and related practices like neuro-linguistic programming, I (and clients) experience the quickest results when facilitating sensory experiences most compatible with dominant learning styles.

Visual (seeing and looking) learners connect most effectively with written information and graphics. When taking notes, using color to highlight subjects and groups of thoughts is highly effective (like creating categories or chunks of data). Visual learners will be interested to know that writing in a lecture or workshop, for instance, is the same as dictating. Once the physical recording process is halted (pencils are not in hand), information can be absorbed and thorough learning takes place. Most would say they are strongest when learning visually.

A friend who went back to school for her masters in accounting was very frustrated and complained, "I don't understand anything during the lecture." I responded, "Do you take detailed notes?" Her response was, "Yes." I suggested that she consider taking a voice recorder into class so she can listen in lieu of dictating, ask questions in real time when she doesn't understand a concept, then take notes when returning home. Or, take notes in the lecture, listen to the recording to absorb more information without taking notes to see if it makes more sense, then ask the instructor follow-up questions via email, phone or before the next lecture commences. In other words, experiment and come up with a process to use more than one style of learning.

Audio (hearing and listening) learners connect most effectively to the spoken word. They tend to listen then transfer what they heard on paper later. If audio learners take notes during a lecture the best way to absorb the information is to read the notes aloud when alone. Listening to voice recordings over and over again cements information into an audio's brain. Audios thrive when all the information they need is covered in spoken lectures which can include formal instruction and discussions with others. This is the second largest learning style (those who consider themselves primarily audio).

Instructors who are visual or tactile learners may perceive students aren't listening if they aren't taking notes, but I mention up-front that if I don't see note takers I assume that they are audio learners, or possibly tactile. One workshop attendee shocked fellow learners when she recited an entire piece of work that she transcribed from a recording (for a natural voice exercise earlier in the program). Another that I recognized upfront as an audio learner was legally blind.

Tactile learners (acquire information through touching and observing movements) must be able to imitate, practice, and experience to their satisfaction. This learning style can be perceived as being slow or tending to procrastinate, but it's more about being hands-on and applying learning. Ultimately, information must be recorded in some way and a tactile will learn most effectively by writing the same information over and over again (even tracing information like maps, tables, and graphics with the physical finger). Generally, they need to know the bigger picture so when they have to dive into details they don't feel their time is wasted. If there were 20 people in a room, only one might consider tactile as her primary learning style.

When working with clients who are primarily tactile and they become frustrated with fine points, they have to be reminded of the reason for dabbling in (what they consider) the minutia. As a facilitator, an effective approach is what is heard from a radio or TV program host, "This is WMAP radio, and we're talking about…." Then the tactile finds ways to stand back and apply information.

The learning curve is drastically increased when acknowledging your number one strength then combining other components to accelerate learning in the number two and three learning style positions. For instance, when I do yoga I can't take instruction by watching the teacher do a pose and listen at the same time. I, generally, choose audio (when I know the pose) or I end up mirroring the instructor (his left will be my right when looking at the instructor in the front of the room) and I hear, "Your other left, Michelle." If a lecturer (in a seminar) is referring to a visual, I make an in-the-moment decision to listen and dictate what I heard (I can read the information later), or read and block audio (the instructor's voice).

My training in neuro-linguistic programming includes understanding eye movements. Here's a very simple crash course. Unless intentionally rehearsed to do otherwise, eye movements provide quick clues on what senses others are pulling from. When eyes roll up, eyes close (to see into the mind's eye), or glaze over and stare straight out into space, those are usually visual patterns. If eyes move side-to-side (or ear-to-ear) this is audio. If eyes drift down toward the waist, or maybe hands are gesturing (unrehearsed) then this is more feeling or tactile. You will also find visuals use words phrases like "*See* what I'm saying?" Audios might ask, "Do you hear where I'm coming from?" Tactiles might say, "I'm just not feeling it. I need to experience for myself." Other subtle words and eye movements tell more of a tale, but I use this knowledge when sensory-based coaching.

Armed with this information, it's time to stretch our writing fingers. As a caveat, be aware that while it's most effective to learn and create to your strength, if you are going public with your work then you should consider polishing and revising to reach all three learning styles.

Self-Portrait Writing and Activating Sensory Experiences

Putting theory to practice, you can create vivid self-portraits. Research has shown that a measurable amount of creativity in word usage is experienced when in a relaxed, hypnotic state (Marinelli, 2012). In addition, overall writing competence is shown to be enhanced when there is a personal connection to text (Perin, Keselman, & Monopoli, 2003). Sensory over-exploring on paper — even though material may not be used later — trains the mind to extend ideas, which then becomes habit. So, my recommendation is to continue writing even when the text seems to be over-dripping detail. The following personal writing example illustrates one way to extend the writing experience with sensory-based recall.

Padding down the fraying, red-stained carpet steps, a filthy film forms on the bottom of my feet. Six in the morning, it's still dark out when I reach the kitchen. I stomp then turn on the light to disturb roaches hunting for morsels so that they scatter to their hideouts. Then I hear rustling in the large wooden wine barrel repurposed to hold trash. Crap! Is it the rat from the basement again?

Gingerly picking up the loaf of bread on the counter top with three fingertips, it's like playing peek-a-boo with cockroaches that made the wrong choice in hide-in-go-seek. Then it was time to fee-fi-fo-fum clomp over to the cupboard while intermittently gazing behind me — on alert if the rat swims its way to the top of the sea of garbage and makes a run for it. I knock on the door encouraging mice to scatter, gently tug on the age-warped, six-panel wooden door and peek in. They are there — plenty of tiny, brown, droppings to prove that — so it's best not to dawdle. I snatch a box of cereal then slam the door closed. Not out of the woods yet, it's prudent to check the bag to make sure it's secured before pouring the goods into the bowl. There's nothing worse than walking through the pest mine field only to find unwanted items floating in your milk.

Every now and then I pretend we live in a tidy, functional home that a family takes pride in. This requires a fair amount of work on my part, however. During one attempt to build my dream world, I decide to pull all food out of the kitchen pantry and freestanding cupboard and disinvite non-rent paying vermin. Using an aerosol can of chemicals I drench the shelves with a toxin that likely shortens my life as well.

This is the day I learn that cockroaches can fly as a long, slender, brown insect takes flight out of a cabinet. I simultaneously suck in air, screech then experience a burning sensation in my throat as I swallow bug spray. Disgusted I crunch the soaring creature once it hits the floor. Too late to turn back, I soak everything with soap and water then return foodstuff to their original places.

I don't remember being acknowledged for a job well done this time or for others. I'm not even sure anyone notices. Recognition is less my goal and more about experimenting with what it's like living in a clean, healthy environment. It's like *playing* house, but it also comes with a price in my run-down neighborhood with echoes of "What, you think you're better than us?"

This is a self-coached, silent written piece by me. While only part of the essay is provided, what I most enjoyed was the icky aspect — if typing stopped, I got gross. There are a number of places where I could extend the experience by asking in the moment questions, "What am I hearing, seeing, smelling, tasting, and feeling?"

With enough self-questioning and what I term bridging in hypnosis (to get closer to the truth or, at least, my perception of the truth), I can develop the story through recall and close guessing. This familial, nonfiction, expressive recall creates a flow factor in writing that can be applied consistently to extend writing practices. This can be expanded to the sciences, contribute to scholarship, clarify protocol, and business communication as well.

Expanding Laboratory Work with Sensory-Based, Oral Storytelling

Sensory writing and science? What? Let's break a paradigm. While science based work encourages a more dissociative voice, this coaching session begins in the first person with a personal approach to develop content.

Coach (C): I'd like you to remember an experiment. Where would you find yourself? What would you find yourself doing?... What's the beginning for you?

Lab Technician (LT): The beginning would be when I pull samples.

C: ...Tell me the first thing that you're going to do?

LT: You thaw it.

C: You go to get it where?

LT: From the minus 80 freezer.

C: Tell me about the minus 80 freezer. Tell me what happens when you go into that freezer.

LT: ...Most of the samples are in boxes and racks. You have to get like special gloves so you can grab the sample because it's really cold...

C: How does minus 80 feel?

LT: It's pretty cold, but not as cold as nitrogen which is minus 150....

Note: More descriptions followed on the freezer experience that is not included, but this is a way to gain rapport and evolve to a sensory, imaginative mode.

C: So what's next...? You're moving into the experiment time. Tell me about that.

LT: So, I bring in the samples and I usually set them on the counter to let them thaw out a room temperature, and then I'll go grab my protocol for DNA extraction… then I hang up my protocol.

C: …So what do you do?

LT: I can't give you the exact protocol.

C: …Tell me what's happening once your sample thaws. What's happening?

LT: Well, a lot of cells die when it thaws. That's why you don't want to do a lot of freezing and thawing. You usually just want to thaw it once.…

C: Okay, so you're going to use a little sample. What do you do?

LT: I can't remember the protocol.

C: Don't go to the protocol, tell me what you're going to see. Do you see something in a microscope?

LT: …I see a tube full of red liquid because there are a lot of red blood cells in it. I have to lyse the red blood cells — that's one of my first steps. So first I grab all of my reagents… I'm going to use and lay them all out on the counter… any tubes that I need… I'll label those… I lyse red blood cells and the neutrophils, then you do a couple wash steps, then we do DNA precipitation and in the end you end up with your DNA.

C: What's that look like?

LT: It's just clear. It's actually really cool when you precipitate the DNA.…

C: Describe that.

LT: It's done with just ethanol. I think 95% ethanol. You'll take the liquid that you know the DNA's in and put that into the 95% ethanol, invert it a couple of times, and then you actually see the strings of DNA start to develop.

C: What does that look like?

LT: Usually like creamy color, stringy, and then the more you invert it, depending on how much is there, it will start to clump. And then if there's a lot it will just look like a giant creamy clump on the bottom. But, if there's only a little bit it will look just like little cool strings hanging out in the ethanol.

C: So tell me more about the colors. How does that look?

LT: It's mostly just cream colored. There are some that are brownish, but I'm not sure why. They're all, pretty much, cream colored.

C: So what did you say about the shape, their strings?

LT: Yeah. They're DNA strands so it makes sense that their stringy. I think they start to clump because of hydro [...] I can't think of the term.

C: That's okay, you don't have to name that right now. So, you said there are DNA strands. Why do you think that's cool?

LT: Just because it's the foundation... one of the smallest units of life, the smallest aspect of life. I can visualize, I can see it in the tube which is really, really cool....

C: Do you know what that looks like in a small telescope?

LT: I actually don't know that I have... but we always looked at pictures of it... the double helix DNA.... We know what the model looks like in a way that you would never be able to see with your naked eye....

C: How long do you get to see that creamy string?

LT: It depends on the sample.... If there's a lot of DNA, it goes away really quick so it will just clump up real quick. If there's not that much DNA some of it doesn't really stick together so the strings will kind of hover in the solution. But either way, you're not supposed to let it sit in that step for too long… so we usually spin it down pretty soon after that, and then it pellets down at the bottom and just forms a chunk of DNA at the bottom of the tube.

C: So what does that look like?

LT: That's kind of boring compared to the cool stringy stuff. It's just like little pellets — a little round pellet at the bottom. Sometimes it's big, sometimes it's really tiny, sometimes you can't see it at all because there's such a small amount of DNA.

C: So then what happens after that?

LT: After that we do a couple wash steps with ethanol, and then again. And then I think we add our hydration solution.

C: When you do a wash, what does that mean?

LT: That basically just means adding… something that just kind of takes away the gunk from the pellet that you're looking at… Sometimes that's just a salt solution… it coaxes out some of the bad stuff, and then when you spin it down again, the denser DNA is going to pellet down at the bottom and then the gunk you don't want… is going to hover in the… liquid above the pellet… When I work with saliva samples there's a lot more DNA and you can really see it.

While the laboratory coaching is in natural written voice and first person, it can be changed in polish stage to a more formal voice. This was only a small part of the edited interview, and there were a number of areas that could have been further explored depending on the goal of the finished product. The laboratory technician did reflect afterwards that certain details covered would have saved time and decreased stress had she read another technician's transcription to follow certain protocol (look for…, expect to see…). These types of in the moment, reimagined exercises (Balgopal, Meena, & Wallace, 2013) have been shown to contribute to technical writing that enhances the ability to more precisely understand experiments which then can contribute to details and discoveries for published papers, or other academic work.

The added lesson with the science exercise is similar to what Peter Elbow discusses in *Vernacular Eloquence*. Regardless of how technical the subject, when he asks a struggling student to summarize what she has written it can be articulated aloud with clarity, but when reading the standard written English or silent written rendition it can be like reading a completely different, indistinguishable paper. Crossbreeding concepts and putting writing concepts into a personally relatable context progresses story telling (orally and in writing). Revising verb tenses and first, second or third person can be changed during the editing phase.

Expressive Writing to Relieve Test Anxiety

Then there are situations where revision is non-existent. The answer is standard. Period. The anticipation of failure that accompanies these types of circumstances can be crippling and creates emotional anxiety that can even lead to physical ailments if left unattended.

Returning to graduate school in my late 40's and early 50's I found myself more inwardly competitive than in undergraduate school — I wanted that "A" on my transcript so internal pressure would build at times. Upon personal reflection, situations where I didn't test or complete an assignment with an exemplary grade had a lot to do with not understanding the process or instructions.

Formal writing and reading have been connected to feeling out of one's natural element in research mentioned earlier. In contrast, writing freely (with no concern for punctuation, structure, or spelling) and reading for entertainment can create relaxation, even liberation. In the Frattaroli, et al (2011) study, it's clear that those taking certain high-stakes exams have found relief and even achieved better grades when expressively writing about their duress connected to test taking. Maintaining composure during the test (reading instructions and answering with confidence), self-hypnosis tools can be added to remain or re-instate calm — similar processes to imagery coaching (Frey, 1980) in the classroom, and calming university students prior to a project (Martinez, Kock, & Cass, 2011)

Extending this concept to my mind over matter solutions practice, clients have increased the likelihood of relaxing while responding to questions in standard entrance or exit exams. But, before I go into the details, be clear this is not magic. You have to roll up your sleeves to prepare for tests by:

- studying the anticipated material on the test;
- having knowledge of the test format – multiple choice or essay, number of questions, time allotment, practice tests (which may even include failing and retaking);
- and knowing something about the testing environment is helpful — computer room, classroom, office, tables or desks, natural light, etc.

Sensory Step One. Moving into the details of how to create calm in stressful situations, re-live simple examples like when you learned to drive a stick shift, completed a challenging craft, or conquered a video game level. Get as sensory detailed as possible to remember all the good stuff (see, taste, smell, hear, feel). You don't have to save the world, just relive the success. If you want your experiences to be specific to testing, understand what goes through your mind when you are certain of the answer in a testing experience. What's important is that you reuse the avenues in the brain to remind you that you have effectively moved from stress to calm.

Sensory Step Two. Once you have retraveled through six or so positive memory avenues, you can visualize what goes through your mind when in test stress (only one example is fine as human beings are prone to go on and on about what's wrong). Limit the recall detail to remain in a balanced state.

Sensory Step Three. Choose the strongest sensory experience of moving from stress to calm. Get into every detail of the accomplishment experience (how the body moves, tone of voice, facial expressions) so that your brain can re-access that experience immediately. Recall test stress then immediately switch to success. To create the highest sensory recall experience of success (see, feel, smell, hear, etc.) reference the *Sensory-Based Writing Framework* section to use visualization (which is story retelling), writing, and reading aloud so it cements success into the memory. The result is you are training your mind when in test stress to automatically switch to accomplishment.

Great. So now you know how to anchor success, but you also need to know the information that is going to be on the test. Gee's (2007) premise is that recalling information is accessed most easily through association — something connected to your life — rather than stuffing material in the mind and hoping memory will serve when under pressure. Taking a little time up-front to associate with material so that you can relate to it personally will pay off. A chiropractor shared how amusing it was during her final exam with students moving limbs and observing them as if looking through the skin to muscles, tendons, and bones.

Refer to the *What Type of Writer and Learner are You?* section so you are clear on how you recall information. My number one sense is visual so

I will recall how and where I've written something on paper during an exam for a certain amount of time. But, I (or we, if Gee is correct) can only commit information to memory forever if I associate information to my life.

A testing experience, then, might look like the following:
- you've studied,
- you know how much time you have to answer each question to pace yourself,
- sitting down to take the test you feel stress, but you know your process to re-create calm,
- you begin the test and know the answer. Success!
- you go to the next question and panic — "Crap! I don't know the answer!"
- you mark that answer to symbolize to come back to the question after adding successes,
- you take 10-20 seconds — seeing this on paper it may seem like a small amount to time, so time it for yourself to see how it feels — to recall confidence felt with the established success anchor (established prior to the exam),
- you are ready to look at the next question,
- you read to the next question and know the correct answer. Success!

The formula isn't exact, but most elements are present, so customize to taste. In my practice I recommend expressive writing in session with follow-up writing one week to ten days prior to the exam. To maximize releasing anxiety consider reading your thoughts aloud (alone or with someone present is fine). To strengthen your confidence in the ability to answer questions accurately, rehearse what a testing experience might look like — this creates familiarity and gives you a sense of security (be sure to gather potential test data to get the most out of the experience). To truly own that you have plenty of time to finish and receive an exemplary grade, minutes per question should be timed — this includes minutes per successful answer, as well as minutes per process of elimination answer. All of the above can be done on your own or with a facilitator.

On the big day, *be* in the testing room. Think only about that moment and how to retrofit your preparation with what the standard exam is asking.

On my high-stakes exam day, my stomach was in knots prior to entering the room, but I was composed when I sat down to begin the test. I was prepared. When studying for my final comprehensive exam in graduate school (required to pass in order to be awarded my masters degree), my best guesses on what the questions might be were not exactly the same (of course) as the actual exam. I knew that I understood the fundamental elements, however. I was clear that the format would be essay questions only, how much time I had per question, I would be typing my final answers on the computer, and I could bring water and paper to jot down thoughts. The first ten or so minutes of the exam I reviewed all questions (I allotted this time when rehearsing), I reorganized key points on paper that I studied to address each question, entered the details into the computer, and had time to stand up and stretch while proofreading. I passed.

To be clear, the Frattaroli, et al (2011) study, asked the students interested in entering law school and medical school to independently write about their deepest thoughts and feelings nine days prior to the upcoming exams and their scores were higher than those who didn't do the same exercise. No sensory-based coaching. No visualization prior to and during the exam time. The additional exercises are for those interested in multiple mind over matter processes along with academic focus.

Sensory-Based Tools For Self-Help

ORDINARY WRITING TO SOOTHE THE SOUL

Connecting some of the dots in research with sensory-based writing and storytelling out loud, expressive writing created an altered consciousness for graduate students taking high-stakes exams (Frattaroli, Thomas, & Lyumbomirsky, 2011). Expressive writing showed higher levels of well-being psychologically and socially including less depression and anxiety that created more meaning and enjoyment in life (Bhullar, Schutte & Malouff, 2011).

With ordinary voice, releasing academic barriers to writing — standard written English and punctuation in exercises, for instance — personal storytelling is a tool for well-being. Let's be clear in the world of storytelling that there is an on-paper rendition, but audio learners could play to their strengths with voice recording being their final products. Visuals may voice record as a brainstorming tool then silent write. Tactiles may draw the big picture — in essence, summarize the final page of the story — then provide more extensive information in other visual or audio ways.

For instance, a painter and photographer, and (now) family friend, went to college but didn't do very well in that type of structured environment. His artist statement shared that he learned his craft through trial and error (strong tactile traits). While I own a couple of pieces of his work, I was most attracted to a piece that he called *Fin* (in French this is a derivation of the verb "to finish"). When viewing *Fin* on the wall, one would never guess what it really means, but this painting was about his history: the original painting on this canvas addressed how he struggled within himself, with friends, family, and his lover so it was very dark — he hated the piece; a couple of years later he was happier and ripped off certain layers of the canvas and painted who he had become and came to love the piece. Both he and his work are wonderfully layered. From my perspective, we all move through these stages at some point in our lives. As a tactile, I requested that he write an imperfect explanation of *Fin*, in ordinary language, so that he would be comfortable sharing his thoughts (not that it would be any easier for professional writers who may seek perfection with every word and punctuation mark, but I've already explained my thoughts on natural voice). I treasure his explanation.

There are numerous options that can combine all learning styles, but the following are some scenarios that I might use in workshops and one-on-one scenarios.

Sensory-Based Writing and Beginning at the End

Writing is like playing an instrument or training for a marathon, you have to practice to improve, become fluid and confident in your movements. One of the exercises that I used in a workshop is begin at the end. Each writer chooses a slice of life picture like the following.

Sensory-Based Tools For Self-Help 61

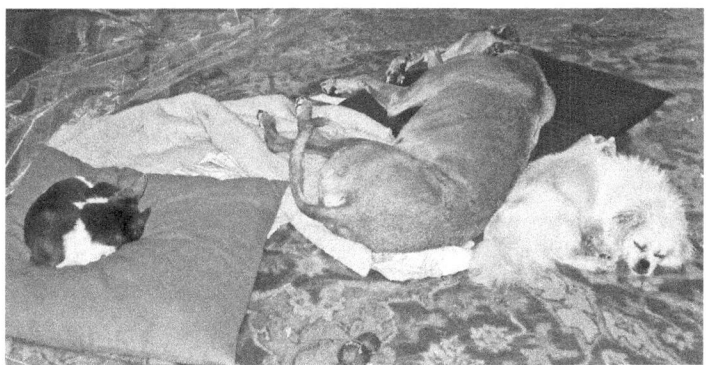

The assignment is then to tell a story about the picture. The ground rules are: use present tense (be in the moment, as if in the scene), no punctuation or spelling rules apply, use ordinary voice.

Silent writing or image telling aloud, jump into the photo and what are the sounds and aromas associated with the scene? Who are the people or animals? What are they doing at the moment? Why are they doing what they are doing?

What occurs prior to the photo? How did they work up to that scene? How do they feel prior to the photo being snapped?

Fast forward. What are they moving toward, after the photo is taken? Why? What are the sights, sounds, colors, aromas, emotions connected to the extended story?

Now get really silly. Over extend the story to the point of fantastic, supernatural, outlandish.

Why not look at one of your own photos? Recall details of the scene, prior to the scene, and after the scene. Stretch your senses by thinking about the environment, the colors, smells, and emotions.

Exercises like these are like playing the scales on a piano, or swimming laps in a pool — working your way into the larger body of work. If you feel like you don't have as much time to practice, get practical. Associate a visual with what you want to accomplish in your current writing project. For instance, when I was writing about *Your selfie voice* at the beginning of this book, I used this photo for clarity to tap and retap into the moment of what selfie means today and in this context.

Before moving into the standardizing mindset push yourself to the limit, take a break, then push yourself again. Get sloppy and ridiculous then review the *Sensory Framework* section to be reminded of how to build even more content, as well as suggestions when moving into polish stage.

EXPRESSIVE WRITING AND FOCUSING ON ADVERSITY OPPOSITES WHEN TELLING YOUR STORY

It is tempting to focus on the negative and how someone did you wrong because it's so highly charged — anger advances many senses, but being upset encourages the mind and the body to replay the terrible situation over and over again (especially when justifying seeking revenge). We've been trained since children with classic stories from *Snow White*, and *Beauty and the Beast*, to *Pride & Prejudice* to pinpoint a villain, hero or heroine, and a victim. When retelling a story, if the hero isn't your role then you must be the victim. Rarely does one rehash a story where she is the villain.

When in a mind over matter (sensory-based) session, one problem (the primary theme aloud or thesis on paper) is established — for example, romantic love relationship issues. The mind and the body will only truly believe in itself if it can reassociate with past successful experiences (as Gee, 2007, would suggest and I concur). Our brains are, basically, a bunch of energetic roads. There are roads that are energetically labeled successful and pleasing experiences. There are roads labeled the opposite. Creating a scenario, let's say someone was married several times and has decided she has a problem with being a bad partner picker. There had to be times when she was a good picker in some type of relationship, however.

Each relationship was selected for positive reasons at certain points in time, and those points in time are what she would relive through sensory-based work (also called visualization, hypnosis, or self-hypnosis). Building the story, assume her first marriage was at 18 years old — ah, the memories that come with young love — to a smart young man who would go on to work in the family business, and she would stay at home and take care of the kids. She gets bored, has problems with the parents, feels trapped, and leaves. There were snippets, however, when the relationship was fulfilling. Moments of satisfaction would be jotted down on paper (at first, a short sentence only). The recaller might move into, "yeah, but…" and that's when the recall brakes are applied (stick with the good stuff for this exercise).

Then there is a whimsical elope (the second marriage experience). There were reasons why this was a good idea at the time and those would be jotted down. Then the third, and longest, marriage snippets would be jotted down (the please-let-this-work-this-time union). Generally speaking, six to 12 experiences are quickly recorded on paper. Perspective begins to be replaced even with little sensory work due to the number of successful "I didn't think of it that way," and "I always looked at the final outcome as the ultimate failure" thoughts.

Next step is to go back and visualize all the sensory data that comes with each positive experience aloud. I ask the recaller to share details of the story that include (in the present and first person): what she looks like, what is she wearing (if she doesn't remember, recall what she could be wearing) and how does it feel on the body (is a garment hugging certain parts of her body, how are her feet configured), what do her hands look like, how does her hair feel, what does the room look like, the furniture, the smells associated with the experience, and other sensations.

With each experience, the perspective on the problem begins to shift slightly.

- Once reexperiencing all points in time, the recaller ranks the top three experiences of what is most vivid, easy to remember and connect with.
- Return to the original problem — choose a strong experience associated with the issue — recall is redirected to the top positive (opposite) experience including: tonality, body language, internal thought, words used, and other senses.
- Return to the negative issue (in the mind's eye) then return to how body and mind movements were handled differently (positive, opposite), with confidence in the past.

- Return to the issue, return to the opposite — the success. Then cement in the details of success from the past and how this can be repeated by recalling that accomplishment over and over and over again (also a form of neuro-linguistic re-programming — creating a renewed perspective by re-associating reality).

The bottom line is if you can create the same mistake over and over again, you can create success over and over again. You retrain your mind and body to be your own hero.

With or without a facilitator, these exercises can be executed aloud, or through silent writing. Polish can come later if the goal is to publish, or this can simply be a private reflection exercise.

Writers' Brainstorming Process

WHAT TO WRITE ABOUT

While I enjoyed writing, my undergraduate degree wasn't in English studies but in Communication Arts. I viewed writing as more of a promotional tool — writing advertising copy, product and service stories in corporate newsletters, brochures, and electronic verbiage for websites. Writing books was never on my radar screen. I didn't feel like I had anything interesting to say.

But then I began to reflect on what it meant to live in poverty and dysfunction, how I felt like I didn't fit in anywhere, and the resentment I felt as a result. My first book — *Adventures of a Mainstream Metaphysical Mom: Finding Peace of Mind in a World of Diversity* — was basically journaling. It wasn't until I generated about a hundred or so pages and was reading it aloud to my inner circle that I mustered up the courage to self-publish.

Once published I thought there would be a series of *Mainstream Metaphysical Mom* books only, but other books popped into my head as I continuously learned new subjects, taught workshops and saw clients. Unknowingly, a common theme that has emerged with all my work is, "you are the boss on how you fit." And I realized that as soon as I settle in (at any given time), I seem to test my fitness.

When returning to academia for a Master's in English, I felt a familiar "what the hell am I doing here?" fire in my belly — I didn't fit. I resented those who were creating rules to generate groupthink, yet every seminar I completed in grad school brought me new aha moments in how my mind over matter and wholistic and integrative work complemented my academic studies. Bringing the two together, *Writing Sensorably* was born, but this took years of experiences and brain percolation (jotting little ideas on paper, testing concepts with clients and students, and chatting with others) to figure out how the puzzle pieces could be connected on paper.

In the *Studies at-a-Glance* and the *Framework* sections, writer's block is addressed, but there is no detail on subjects to write (or talk) about. I covered *Expressive Writing and Focusing on Adversity Opposites when Telling Your Story* and used an example connected to love interests as a kickstart to this practice, but to get creative juices flowing we will look at some self-coaching processes and other writing concepts. Remember to jot down your own ideas as you move through this next section.

What's the Problem?

This section is for one who needs a little push on the value of her words. The problem will be "I don't have anything ground breaking to talk or write about." The opposite of this is "I have interesting information to share." To be a bit more visually appealing, here is a more direct layout.

Problem in-the-moment:
  I don't have anything ground breaking to talk or write about.

Opposite experience:
  I have interesting information to share — aloud and visually.

Using mind over matter recall to overcome the mentioned problem, you should consider looking at any time in your life when others have been interested in what you have to say. The first question to answer is how far back do you remember life events? Triggers or anchors to self-indicate how far back in grade school (K-12) you recall information include: teachers that made impacts, groups of friends, sports played, activity involvement, and houses you've lived in, for instance. The key is to adhere to the theme, thesis, or subject of "I have interesting information to share." Remember to see through your eyes at that time ("I am...") while reexperiencing (be there again). Initially, these are short thoughts that will be experienced in more detail later. Closing your eyes isn't necessary to recall information. I will begin closer to my age now then work my way to younger ages because this is the way I am thinking today (can be done in any order that works for you).

THEME:

I have interesting information to share — aloud and visually.

TIME-LINING:
- 40-50 something years old. Leading a monthly community meeting, I found balance that gave others' voices as well as my own. Less is more, and leading by example with kindness and gentle boundaries became even a clearer lessons.
- 30-something years old. When I transitioned to no longer being the President of a trade association as an adult professional, I had to let go of being heard when certain financial decisions were being made. I was no longer the boss, essentially.

- Late teens, Early 20's. When in college I was the Vice President of a student organization and got member's attention. During one meeting I realized that I was being intimidating to make members do what I wanted them to do.
- Late teens. When I was in college a guy hit the back of my car (with his car) and ran. When I reported the hit and run, the detective was very interested in what I had to say. When we went to court the judge was very interested in what I had to say. It was a big lesson on less is more — be careful how long-winded you get even when you are completely in the right.
- When I was in high school there was a robbery at my workplace, and the top manager asked me to come into his office downtown and share what I knew.
- I was s supervisor in high school at the Lunken Airport Playfield and people my age had to listen to me. This was the first time I could differentiate between people wanting to listen to me and when they were forced to due to my position. This is also my first lesson on being too power hungry.
- I was the announcer in sixth grade for the talent show in elementary school.
- Fifth or sixth grade. My friend, Sandra, and I wore tank tops underneath our clothes and when we went out onto the playground we took off our legal school attire to show our tank tops to protest the boys having a kick ball playground because girls weren't permitted.

Eight short examples then lead into more detailed sensory-based recall. On a personal note, as a writer this is where I will become insecure as I am going to freewrite this excerpt without punctuation (using only a random character or a period if I just can't help myself) so you can see how the framework I describe at the beginning of this book plays out.

SENSORY-BASED DETAILED PROBLEM SOLVING

The concept is when you reexperience the solution to the problem today, the body and mind can readopt the patterns. Reassociation creates resuccess. I will recall (through silent, sensory-based writing) my experience in a court room as a teen (freshman in college to be exact). My eyes were closed as I typed (versus handwriting) for some of the time so I didn't know where the asterisk was and used the period to keep my mind and fingers moving. Every now and again I couldn't keep myself from using punctuation that felt really obvious, I stayed away from anything more than a period or comma, but didn't permit myself to evaluate whether the marks were correct.

> I sit in a type of box. It seems like a throne made of drywall. White paint. Wood finish on the top and I can rest my arms on them like a queen on her throne. I think there are two steps to walk into the box and it's covered by a carpet on the floor and internal walls. There is a simple chair inside the box like something I would find in a classroom. Somehow that makes things feel a bit less intimidating. I am wearing my regular student clothes. Really a bit shabby, but I'm only 18. What do I know.
>
> The guy who hit me is an African American. He is in good physical shape. His face is clean shaven and his hair is shaved really close. He wears a sharp suit and decides he is going to be his own lawyer. He begins grilling me with questions like I was at fault for him hitting my car then giving me false information. Luckily the detective asked me detailed questions prior to the

court date and I told him the car was a hatchback, it had a bunch of *Cincinnati Enquirer* newspapers, there was a younger, African American boy with him. That's all the detective had to go on, and we still have our guy.

So, anyway, the guy that hits me decides to act like a lawyer that he might have seen on TV. He writes this graphic on a white board and shows our cars and starts grilling me to try to confuse me. My heart begins to beat a bit harder and I find myself becoming angry. Before I allow him to confuse the situation I say, "Look. You hit me from behind. You lied about who you were and then you left. It's pretty straightforward." I knew I should stop there. Getting angry or self-righteous would have hurt my case. And then all I remember is everyone stopping — the detective, the wanna-be TV lawyer guilty of hitting and running guy, and even the judge.

We meet outside the courtroom and the detective came out and said, "You did good. We'll let you know about next steps."

I could have sensory-expanded in a number of areas — more of the courtroom, what I was wearing, what the defendant was wearing, what the defendant wanna-be-lawyer said, more on the scene of the crime, the detective's description — but I got to the crux of the matter from a mind over matter perspective and stopped there. I shared applicable information that resulted in the entire court room listening. I got to the point, remained on the subject, and controlled my indignation. I can re-associate with that memory to re-train myself. In a full session (or when self-analyzing) all experiences in the timeline would be expanded on, and then the top one to three (sometimes more depending on the situation) would be used as neuro-linguistic reprogramming anchors as reminders of past accomplishments.

Once finding patterns of remembering that I have had important things to say (the proof being others' listened) then I could move onto another subject, thesis, theme like, "I have written best when...." I could describe environment, time of day, length of time, and other habits that prepare my mind, body and spirit to plant text on the screen.

Writing On Passionate Subjects

READING TO WRITE AND SPEAK

I wasn't an avid book reader growing up unless it was required in school. I'd read a few books for fun here and there, but I loved comic books, movie star magazines, and television in my teens. When I received my undergraduate degree I vowed to never read another book, so it wasn't until I was in my 30's that I began to listen to (while making long commutes to work) and read books not required for business. Writing outside of commercial applications (magazine and newsletter articles, and copywriting, for examples) didn't occur to me until I got involved in the self-help industry. As my writing progressed so did my reading — for fun as much as for work. If I'm writing self-help, I usually read material that has little to do with the same subject during leisure time. However, reading of fiction (for instance) still stimulates how to effectively use the natural voice, as well as punctuation.

I can't recall attempting to sound out words to comprehend reading and grammar usage when I was a child, but I can recollect the humbling experience of working toward becoming confident in French in my 40's and 50's (which included studying abroad to immerse myself in the culture and language). Memorization didn't work unless I could put the words into context that applied to me (there was little reason to remember the word "liver" if I didn't eat, operate on, or have problems with that organ). Associating words with pictures facilitated the process initially, and then in more advanced work I followed stories with limited pictures and looked for ways to apply the content to things that I might use daily. Certain punctuation might provide hints that information is connected (a colon prepares me for a listing of related information, for instance), but I have to know most of the vocabulary to understand why certain marks are used.

The point is that consistent observing results in acting out similar patterns (much more hands-on than memorizing a rule only). Reading becomes a type of effortless learning. So, to put content into action that you might connect with, the following pages are examples of subjects you may be interested in writing about or these subjects may stir up other ideas. The following is putting linear instruction into action — combining my personal examples connecting the natural voice that accompanies sensory-based writing with the research and framework covered in the earlier sections.

Adversity as Building Blocks

RECALL. Five, maybe six years old, my eyes shoot open while my baby sister dozes next to me. We hover above the floor like boat over deep water. The bed so large, to us, that we both can spread our arms and legs wide and oscillate as if making sand angels on the beach. The headboard rests against the wall common with the door and allows me to peer into the goings-on in the lit hallway even though I should be sleeping. But how can I possibly sleep tonight?

I hear a blood curdling scream. Was that my mother? Bare, full breasts and hips with long, auburn Rapunzel hair flashes past my room and out the front door. An echo of screeches follow and then my door shuts tight with a command "Go to sleep, Michelle!"

It wasn't until I was in my forties that I mentioned this memory to my mother. "I didn't know you remembered that" her voice revealing the temptation to deny the past. "What happened?" I inquire. Though forty years had passed the memory was vivid.

She explained that our father and his girlfriend had come home during the wee hours of the morning after drinking. Both approached the bed where she slept and she suddenly felt that they were going to kill her. She began to scream, a hand went over her mouth, she escaped and took flight. Bare as a newborn babe, she raced out the door, plunged into the lake behind the house and hid under the dock. It was autumn, leaves covered the frigid water serving as a natural cloak. "They searched for me, but they thought I drowned," she expanded.

Whether her perception was reality or not, no authorities were called, the scheming lovers left the scene and my brother (seven years my senior, just a teenager) was left to keep watch over us while we slept. I didn't witness our sopping wet and terrified mother return once she sensed it was safe. But, even as a young child, the girlfriend and smell of alcohol created an internal alarm — an anchor to be on full alert, to know my escape routes.

Lessons later in life. Early in my professional work (early 20's and 30's age) in advertising and public relations, it was brought to my attention that I regularly looked for the silver lining in situations. Some were irritated by my "everything happens for a reason" attitude (some would counter with "just admit it's a bad situation"). But, at an early age, to keep my sanity, this was my route to freedom (instead of doing drugs or drinking for an escape). It doesn't mean we are pleased to be in harm's way, but it is about how we choose to view experiences in our lives.

For balance and sanity, I continuously replace my mindset — even with the smallest matters — and decide that even the most negative experiences (adversities) serve a purpose. My choice is not to look back and lament, "If I had to do that all over again...."

I intentionally don't add the word "higher" to this thought, because it makes everything sound so grand. What moves us through life are everyday (many times very subtle) building blocks: little or no decisions, split second turns, a quick nonverbal, a word or phrase.

This is a mindset, a nondenominational thought. It's very easy to push back on this type of idea, especially when something terrible has happened, a dreadful person continues to do appalling things, or you have been victimized. Even if it is crystal clear that you are not at fault, notice how it feels when you view experiences as building blocks.

Childhood Trauma

Recall. It was the late 1960's or very early 1970's. I was early elementary age.

Two story wooden steps lead down to a dirt yard — a dusty soil that leaves dirt lines in and around our noses if we breathe in too deeply that also doubled as a sandbox when we are allowed to play outside. Shredding grey wood picnic tables — about a half dozen — serve the bar clientele next door. Both Mom and Dad's girlfriend wait tables at the bar.

It's a warm day. The door is open to allow for a cross breeze to move from the living room windows through the screen door on the opposite side of the apartment. My sister is in a diaper and I'm in white, cotton panties, neither of us are wearing shirts and shoes to stay cool.

"Let go, Link!" we hear through the screen door of our apartment above the bar and grocery. My sister and I run to the door and begin to scream, "Mommy!" A group of men surround our father lunging like an animal — some pulling on his arms, others his torso — as our mother falls backwards as his long fingers grip her throat. Drunk and enraged, he slurs and growls simultaneously. We continue to reach for the door while our father's girlfriend averts our eyes as we sob, "Daddy, stop!"

My next memory is being in the car with my mother. Her neck — once elegantly displayed in costumes from *Swan Lake* and other classical ballets — is bruised in the shape of his vice-like fingers. Her voice is a whisper from the damage to her vocal cords. Only a few years later, we would comprehend — at least, in the state of Ohio — that the police could not protect our family from domestic violence.

LESSONS LATER IN LIFE. The physical battles would end only after our father was completely ejected from our lives, but the emotional scars would be processed over many more decades. The key was to break the chain. Anger would sear into my mind well into my 30's, but the violent history would not be repeated in my household.

Writing was part of my calming pattern. It was a way of voicing my anger, frustration, judgment, and aggression. It wouldn't be until the early 2000's (in my 30's and 40's) that I would understand the therapeutic power of writing and reading. By 2002, my first self-help book *Adventures of a Mainstream Metaphysical Mom* would be published.

PREJUDICE

RECALL. My father was from Hazard or Perry County, Kentucky. A major coal mining town, my Grandfather (Sizemore) and my father's male siblings (who were much older than he) made their living underground.

My grandmother's maiden name was Campbell and both families were well-known in the region (not always positively with cousins marrying, and the Sizemore boys being hell raisers).

I didn't see much of any of my extended family (on my mother or father's side of the family), but stereotypical Southern prejudices ran their course with my father. We are at an old gas station complete with paint peeling gas pumps. I was maybe five or six years old. It's a beautiful, sunny, spring day when we visit rural Kentucky. My dad demonstrates how to add a pack of salty peanuts into a Coke bottle then drink the soda and eat peanuts simultaneously. Combining the nuts in the bottle, a "hisssssssssss" coupled with tiny bubbles rushing quickly to the surface makes me giggle.

"Drink it and make sure you get some peanuts," he says with a grin. I pour the new found country delicacy in my mouth and pause when he commands, "Chew it!" I crunch, "Mmmmm," enjoying the sweet and salty experience. Taking my next sip, I overhear my dad making monkey squeaks. My mom whispers, "What are you doing?" He snickers low enough for only her ears, while looking at an African American infant being held by her mother, "I'm trying to communicate." This was my first vivid experience of prejudice connected to my father. It wasn't on TV. It. Was. My. Father.

I lived in poor areas that were primarily Caucasian throughout my K-12 schooling years, and didn't make acquaintances with a wider variety of cultures and economic backgrounds until I was a teenager. Being a "have not," I craved getting one step closer to the "have" world so I asked my mom if I could go the private Catholic high school where the rich kids attended. It was a financial stretch, but she found the money. I had a relatively successful junior high school experience: member of the gymnastics and volleyball teams, and President of Student Government.

With some confidence under my belt, surely I could find my niche in a new setting (even as a minority).

Uniforms were worn so it made it easier to fit in, but then nonuniform Fridays were decreed. Fashions separating the rich from the poor burned into every student's memory. It wouldn't be long before I would be called out on my economic status.

One crisp morning, I am sitting on the cement floor waiting for the first bell to ring to go to my locker. A young man rides his moped to school every morning with the Principal's son — a clear demonstration that they live in the more well-to-do area where the school was located and that his family could afford to provide him a motorized vehicle (at 14 years old). He enters the hallway, looks down at me on the floor and announces loudly, "What is an East End sewer rat like you doing in *this* school!" I look up to see many other students waiting to enter the school then stare down at the ground. This was the riding buddy of the Principal's son, what was I going to do? I remain silent.

It wasn't long after this comment that an old junior high school friend decided to attend the same private school as well. I ask him why he transferred and he says, "It is full of 'N———!' I wasn't gonna survive there!" I thought, "It can't be worse than being here and being poor" so I transferred the following school year to the less homogeneous environment for my last two years of high school.

I played volleyball and participated in Student Government, but groups had been formed and few were quick to welcome me (even though my best friend and neighbor — who called me a snob for going to the private school — attended as well). I decided to run for Student Body President my senior year and a friend (who happened to be African American) said, "Michelle, there's no way you're going to win."

"Why?" I asked.

"You really don't get it, do you?"

"What?" I demanded.

Exasperated he blurted, "Never mind!"

I paused and stared and he finally revealed, "You're white!"

LESSONS LATER IN LIFE. I didn't win the election, but my K-12 experiences weren't supposed to build my confidence by being the center of a group think tank. My experiences, instead, attracted me to the underdogs or oddballs — as a general rule – since I was one of them. I didn't become aware of this until I was in my thirties and one of my managers in corporate America said, "You're always hanging out with the people that don't quite fit in." Come to think of it, my husband even called his group of friends in high school "the misfits."

Today, there are times that I strive too hard *not* to fit in. When I dive too deeply into a nonconformist mode I burrow into energetic solitude and resent life demands until I'm ready to re-emerge. What has happened over time is I have more respect and interest in understanding personal space management (you've got to give to get), and comprehending how people prefer to connect. There are some simple rules of thumb to appreciate each person as an individual (when you have the interest and energy): assume diversity — no one person thinks alike and may simply fake it to fit in; respect some noncompliance — expect different opinions and carefully manage combativeness to create an atmosphere of acceptance; appreciate quirkiness — distinctive behavior makes for great learning and can even add a humorous note to many situations.

Victim

Recall. As a child, we moved around a lot. If I romanticized this, I would say that we adopted my father's nomadic, American Indian patterns. The reality was we were constantly run out of town because my father had a lot of bad habits: alcoholic, scam artist, womanizer, didn't pay rent. Maybe part of the problem was his genes and the other part was his attempt to bury the layers of pain from his youth deep into his subconscious. His medications of choice were usually alcohol, pills and anger. Lots of anger.

Hazy snapshots of where I ate and slept linger in my head: a one-floor brick cottage with a rusty swing set in the backyard across from a tiny church; a farmhouse with a big red barn and cornfield where I once got lost; a lake house with a body of water in our backyard as far as the eye could see; a one-floor house walking distance from a small beach with coarse sand; an apartment in a rough part of the city of Chicago where I played in the hallways or on the black iron fire escape outside our kitchen door; an apartment above an adjoining bar and small grocery store with two-story wood steps; and a one-room apartment in Cincinnati. At five years old, this isn't the end of the list, but the one-room apartment is where we began to lay our roots, and where we didn't flee the city or state.

There were five of us by then: my brother (from a different father) who is seven years older than I; my sister, three years younger; myself; my mom and dad. Our family room includes a not-so-gently used, pull out couch in 1960's plaid tweed, complete with scratchy, pilling fabric. A double bed and chest of drawers fills seventy-five percent of the room. Our audio and visual entertainment equipment includes an approximately 12 inch portable black and white TV, and a record player with a lever to choose 45s or 33s and a handle for convenient carrying.

There is a space the size of an outhouse for a toilet. The bathroom door is thin plywood and has a metal hook and eye inside that you can lock for privacy. The kitchen has a roomy eating area and a giant double sink. We use it for cleaning dishes, clothes and bathing. White-paned windows line the long side of the kitchen wall. It's drafty in the winter, especially when you're wet, but it's saturated with natural light, even on a cloudy day. That, coupled with the cheery yellow walls, creates a warmth all its own. Mom loves yellow walls in the kitchen.

Relocating only a few blocks away, by the time I was in first grade, we upgraded to what our family fondly called "the brown house." The unique design includes asphalt roofing shingles instead of the more common metal or wood siding used in the area. Running my hands across the exterior of the house, it feels rough like Dad's face when he doesn't get a chance to shave for a few days (also one of the signs that he is on a drinking binge).

It has five rooms and two full bathrooms, but the kitchen is cold and uninviting. The floor is like ice with thin, brittle laminate and random cracks from wear. Contributing to the problem are several tall, Victorian style windows that capture no sun and seem to have invisible fans blowing air in from the outside. But, we have more room to stretch, to escape.

In the brown house I save a lot of coins from the tooth fairy, pop bottle collecting and selling pot holders door-to-door. My coin holder has clear glass with a polished metal lid, with male and female hinges on one side for fastening. To revel in my savings accomplishment I spend hours organizing my stash: stacking them by denomination; other times piling them in one dollar increments; building coin houses and driving miniature cars through them. Then, exhausting all my options, the coins return to the transparent vault where a lock as small as my thumb, accessed by a miniature, diary-sized key secures my collection for a later playdate.

My pride and joy sits on a shelf like a trophy next to the doorway so all walking by can immediately admire my growing accomplishment.

My mom asked me if she could borrow my collection for groceries, and said she would pay me back the next week. Nearly seven, I beamed with joy. I felt like a peacock strutting with all its iridescent feathers splayed out. While Mom was true to her word, and even added some interest, weeks later there was a security breach. While still on display, my trophy had lost its shimmer: the dainty lock had been twisted and mangled beyond repair and the sparkle dimmed absent of coins.

Smacked with a wave of confusion, I stare at the remnants in a fog of disbelief. Blocking out possibilities of foul play, wondering if I should have been a better child and not accepted repayment from my mother and mourning the loss all at the same time, my hopeful tone asks, "Mommy, did you need money for groceries again?" Looking away, her voice lowers to a whisper "Daddy needed it and will return it soon." Days turned to weeks and weeks to months and the unfathomable became truth: never returned or discussed again, my dad had stolen from me.

Lessons later in life. While this was the first lesson in my life where money was "borrowed" but not returned, it wouldn't be my last. Even into my 40's I loaned thousands of dollars to others and it would not be repaid (others had as much blatant disregard as my father). Maybe part of the problem was I felt guilty because I had money as an adult and others were in need (I knew what that was like, after all). But, after a half century in this life my steadfast boundary had to become "No." No discussions on past disappointments, no agreements that would be dragged into the court system, no hard feelings because money was not reimbursed. The pattern had to be broken — I had to stop hoping others would heal that wound.

Empowerment

RECALL. With the many rooms in the brown house came larger bills, including utilities or the lack thereof. It turned out that there were ways to work around these issues, even as a second grader.

Turning the porcelain faucet handle, maybe, just maybe, there would be more than the disappointing sound of air pushing through pipes. Not today, our bill hasn't been paid again. And the question formed in my young mind, how can I do my class assignment?

What if I asked a neighbor for water like borrowing a cup of sugar? No, the chatter afterwards would be excruciating. The receptors began firing in my brain, if then, if then, if then… if the abandoned ground floor apartment was safe, then my mission is nearly complete. But, can I walk through the fallen debris, broken remnants of unsupervised kids' play, and rats scuttling around the size of small cats?

Leaving quickly, before I lose my nerve, I reach the unoccupied space, see the rust-stained sink through the doorway and hear a faint "plip." With road runner speed, I race in and out, hugging a plastic, lidless, jug of liquid gold to my chest. Success! Water!

Like a smuggler, I carefully pass my unsuspecting mom as she makes breakfast. Clearly she won't understand the importance of this project. When she laughs she blankets her mouth with her hand to cover her black, grey and yellow stumps and pillowy, crimson gums that struggle to hold her teeth in place.

Taking two steps at a time to the second floor, while still keeping my balance to hoard every drop, I enter the room of no use for weeks — what's a bathroom without water? I softly close the door, the stale metal plumbing smell is sealed in the room and finds its way through my nasal passages and into my taste buds. Thick webby saliva puddles on my tongue, making me want to spit it out as I get one step closer to completing my task.

Recalling my mission, a man in a white jacket enters our classroom with a toothbrush as tall as me and a gargantuan set of plastic, white teeth. My second grade teacher, Mrs. Moyer, announces, "Children we have a dentist in to tell us how to take care of our teeth."

We watch the oversized demonstration, brush our teeth like it's a game, suck on red pills and giggle when bloody looking blotches reveal how careless we were with our tooth brushing assignment, and brush again for good measure. We even receive a gift bag with a new toothbrush and toothpaste that tastes like bubble gum!

Our only assignment, "Make sure you brush your teeth every day." I wonder, "Will everyone have water?"

Deeply satisfied, as the smell of bubblegum fills the bathroom and my new toothbrush emerges into a bowl, my answer is a deeply satisfied, "Yes." That day, "Yes."

Lessons later in life. This was actually a remnant of an essay that I'd written in graduate school and it reveals the importance and even accomplishment that I put on having healthy teeth and gums. It was something that I decided that I could control in life, even at 7 and 8 years old.

One of my ultimate achievements will be that this body takes its last breath with a full set of original teeth. Some may see it as strange, but it doesn't hurt anyone. In fact, one could make the argument that the economy is benefiting from my obsession. My dentist makes a whole lot of dough granting me that wish, and I am healthy (not drawing on healthcare resources due to infection). There I go again justifying my quirkiness.

All I did was fetch a pale of water, but this is a story of being proud of rising above adversity at a young age. Many are surprised at how minor recollections can retain significant positive vibes in the body. Easy enough to test for yourself, think about that successful spelling competition, book report, looking great at a gathering. Redirect yourself back to the positive experience if you drift to "yeah, but things went bad…"

Approaching Highly Charged Situations with Caution

Recall. Only one mile away, by third grade we found yet another place to live. Dad didn't have to drive as much because the neighborhood bar was only a few steps away, just across the street. Mom loved the store front on the ground floor with ten foot showcase windows on either side of double doors where she could sell her antiques and collectibles. We lived upstairs.

There was a small New York style grocery store that we could get to by foot, where the smell of fresh meat coupled with freezer burn lingered in the air. Norm, the store namesake and owner, allowed us to create a tab and settle up monthly. In this neighborhood, government checks were common and they arrived every thirty days, so that became payday for all "IOUs." Mom — a steadfast German that also included Irish blood — made it clear that while things were tight she settled our debts with cash earned from an honest day's work (a motto that Dad could only pretend to embrace until he needed another drink).

The kitchen was like a dank cave. With only one three-foot-wide by two-foot-high rectangular window to the right of the sink, it felt more like a nocturnal habitat. If I tiptoed I could just touch the bottom of the windowsill with my fingertips. Standing on a chair I could get a glimpse outside, but it was pointless and uninspiring as I looked directly at the neighbors' metal siding only a broomstick length away.

Holiday celebrations were simple, but with any festivities young hearts were ready to burst when the hour arrived. One Christmas morning Mom met me and my sister in our bedroom, wrapped her arms around us and shuffled us quietly past the tantalizing presents that made our fingers twitch visualizing shredding the paper to find what was inside. Seating us in the dreary kitchen to have breakfast, we were told to be as quiet as mice. Dad passed out in front of the Christmas tree. We would have to wait.

The meal passed, the day wore on, excitement moved to disappointment then disappointment to a familiar resolve. By early afternoon I sat silently on the floor staring at my dad wishing him awake. While waiting my thoughts drifted: how could he be comfortable on the floor; didn't he know what day it was; what kind of mood will he be in when he wakes up? Maybe he heard the wheels turning in my head, because when he opened his dark, deep set eyes, he winced softly, turned and raised his hand as if blocking a spotlight, and stared back at me. I had his present in my lap as he pressed himself up with one hand and then the other to sit Indian-style.

As he came to, I cautiously placed my gift in his yellow, nicotine-stained, calloused hands and said, "Here's your Christmas present Daddy." Not having a gauge on his temperament, I scooted an arm distance away (better safe than sorry). He paused before unwrapping his annual slippers with the care of a surgeon. Silence was safest on my part, and the few words that he spoke carried a tell tale scent of Cutty Sark and Tareyton cigarettes, "Thank you, sweetie."

LESSONS LATER IN LIFE. This would be my lesson in approaching with caution, how not to trap someone into a corner, and (another lesson on how) to make sure there is an escape route. An extension of this behavior is when I'd attempt to make grumpy people smile or attempt to force them into good moods. Over time I realized that it was up to others to create their realities. If I didn't feel comfortable with the vibe then I'd vacate the area (sometimes in spirit and, if possible, also body). Walking on eggshells became a thing of the past. This meant that I had to control my temper as well so others didn't feel like they were walking on eggshells around me — I've been more successful reaching this in my 50's than in my 30's, but I still have my days.

Simple, Happy Memories

Recall. When I was a preteen, on weekends my mother's workplace was the local antique mall. This metal-walled warehouse had hundreds of spaces separated by glass showcases, card tables and peg board. Booths overflowed with comic books in plastic sleeves, Depression glass, license plates from around the world, vintage clothes, war memorabilia and more. Popcorn, processed cheese nachos, rotisserie hot dogs, and the lunch du jour on toasted, white bread lingered in the air.

I freely roamed the endless indoor square feet of musty collectibles like it was my neighborhood, and regularly stretched a couple of soda bottle collecting dollars into a pile of consumables (a gently used toy, graphic novels, a vinyl record). My wandering would come to an abrupt stop when I hear my mom on the opposite side of the building cackling. It wasn't unusual to hear, "There goes Susie again."

Customers who had never encountered my mom's amplified laugh would look up at the loud speakers on the wall. Was someone too close to the announcer's microphone? Turning in the direction of the chortle, as if a child following a Pied Piper, I glide toward what regular's call *Susie's Booth*.

He he ha haaaaaa rat-a-tat-tatted out into bargain buyers' heaven. A pause and another witchlike *He he ha ha haaaaaa* made the thin walls tremble as attention floated in the originator's direction.

Like a baby duckling responding to the mama duck, I follow the call back to her space filled with misfit tchochkes longing for new homes. Mom's bellow rose and fell with what seemed like a measured tempo on a continuous loop. Many observers wondered, "How can she breathe?"

She enjoyed crossword puzzles, but rarely completed them at the mall because traffic flowed like a freeway in her jovial space. Her outbursts pulled people into her booth like Batman to his signal in Gotham City. "Emergency, something to be joyful about" was her message. Mom always found a reason to be tickled and belted it out like an opera singer to spread the joy. Collectibles scroungers and vendors were entertained by her fits of laughter, and even interrupted buying and selling to explore, "We had to come over and find out what's so funny."

My mom became my laugh out loud model. Seeing this playful and silly side molded the laugh I have today. Making and laughing at others' jokes, telling funny stories, and laughing with bravado helped us deal with catastrophes, large and small, just a bit more lightly.

There were risks to creating a humor enriched environment in the chaos of our lives. I went a bit overboard for a time, and my mom didn't know what to do with my harsher teasing as a teen (I got a little mean-spirited and off-color). Not helping matters, when an adult told an inappropriate joke in my presence, "children are present" reminders were not voiced, and Mom just chuckled. Boundaries would grow as I matured as a result of what was perceived by others as hit or miss wit.

LESSONS LATER IN LIFE. There were times in my life when I made attempts to tone down my laughter, but to no avail. I don't even need an audience. I crack myself up!

While living an extremely dysfunctional childhood, one of my mother's unconscious techniques was to laugh it off (we all had done our fair share of crying). Who would have known that would be one of my pathways to enlightenment?

REFRAMING PERCEPTIONS

RECALL. My fondest memories, even in all the turmoil of childhood, were connected to baking cookies for the holidays. My memory goes back as far as approximately four-years-old (when we lived in a house with a large lake in the back). No matter what was going on in our lives we always baked an exorbitant amount of cookies. This is a good example of memory being fallible because we did this every year and it's not always easy to pinpoint an exact experience.

In my teens, I remember a huge butcher's block that we have in our kitchen. The counter top is about eight feet long and two or more feet thick, and has ridges on the surface from cutting and chopping for multiple decades. Notches are built into the front of the block to hang industrial size sharp objects for quick access.

Pans, bowls, rolling pins, wooden spoons, flour, sugar, nuts, and extracts lined one side of the work space while cooling racks and storage containers for finished product reside on the other. Easiest for me to reimagine are two cookies that we make every year: my grandmother's almond cookie with raspberry jam sandwiched in the middle with lemon frosting; and walnut, thumbprint butter cookie.

I remember with even more accuracy my mom pulling the walnut cookies out of the oven, the smell, her quickly placing the hot pan on the butcher's block and pushing her thumb into each hot cookie. When I help, I remember the heat on my thumb and adding my print in lightning speed so that my skin doesn't blister.

During the holidays, it's likely that we hadn't seen our dad in a few days. The likelihood of him being on a drinking binge and blowing his paycheck is also high. Even that hardship can't cancel or overshadow baking season, especially since we are going to share the fruits of our labor with neighbors and friends.

My mom is an antique dealer so we go to flea markets and garage sales nearly every weekend. Inevitably we find cookie tins to serve as durable, reusable gift tins for our handmade treats. Lining multiple dozens of tins with wax paper, we fill them to the brim to symbolize our personal wishes to have a great holiday.

My heart is warmed every time I deliver a tin to a neighbor, especially unexpectedly. One year, when living in a house next to a foundry that made huge metal parts, my mom tells me to deliver cookies to the grumpy old man with unnatural black hair and pale skin, emaciated with poor posture, and had a mean, pale yellow, Chihuahua (that ended up killing our pet chicken, but that's another story). He sits at his kitchen window and stares out at the street for hours.

"Mom, do I have to, he's so mean and creepy."

"Deliver them, Michelle."

With tin in hand, I hesitantly shuffle over to the old man's house and knock on his door. "Ra, ra, ra, ra, raff," the sheer white door curtain opens part way, he waves with the back of his hand and yells, "Go away!"

"I have some cookies for you."

"I don't want to buy anything!"

"They're a gift. We made them."

He opens the door about foot length, his stick-like arm reaches out the door, he grabs the tin and quickly secures his door.

I hustle back into the kitchen and breathe in fresh cookie aroma. Torturous and motivating at the same time, all cookies must be delivered before we get any treats. Ready for my next assignment, "Did you deliver them?"

"Yes."

"What did he say?"

"He thought I was trying to sell him something. I told him they were free and he took them. When I walked by his window, he was sitting at his kitchen table with the tin open."

LESSONS LATER IN LIFE. To this day, I still make my grandmother's almond cookie (as well as others) every December. I have pictures of my kids covered in flour, licking spoons, and have fond memories of filling their wagon full of cookie tins and delivering them together. One year I was burnt out and said, "I don't think I'm going to make cookies this year." My oldest said, "We have to have cookies!" That was the year that she began baking holiday treats.

I have copies of my grandmother's recipe with my mom's handwritten notes that will be handed down to each of my children. We still reuse our old tins — some have been refilled for more than 20 years. My family knows the reward for returned tins is "I get cookies again this year."

Change, the only Constant

Recall. In the fifth grade I found the perfect family home, literally! My best friend lives only one street away. My sister and I can walk to elementary school. It's at the end of a cul-de-sac and very safe, as long as we don't go near the foundry next door. The hum of machine tooling and the train yard clacking is as soothing as ocean waves, compared with bar and pool hall surprise assaults that regularly break out at all hours of the night where we live right now.

This time, before we even move into the house, we paint every wall, and add new linoleum flooring. Mom cakes two yellow coats of paint in the kitchen that accentuates the abundance of natural light that pours in through the four-paneled window.

Eating, reading, doing homework, playing cards and board games are easy in this kitchen. As a rising preteen, I ritually soak my back in the warmth of the afternoon sun while chatting with Mom as she prepares our meals.

One Saturday, Dad plops down in the chair next to me in his underwear, t-shirt and no socks, and rhythmically stomps his feet left then right — like a fan stomping on the bleachers cheering at a football game — celebrating the achievement of a warm and toasty floor. More rejoicing is just around the corner.

Dad usually holds down a job, but his paycheck doesn't always find its way home due to his lack of control. By the time I am in junior high school my mom works a steady retail job plus sells antiques at markets on the side. Mom, a full-figured woman, is equally supple in all areas of her body. With large bosoms that I hope to inherit when I grow up, round hips, and muscular calves that make it difficult to find boots to fit around them, she carries laundry baskets, antique furniture, and moving boxes as easily as an Olympic weightlifter. Her laugh is as hardy as her goddess curves. She has thick, auburn brown hair that makes her scalp sore if she wears it in a ponytail for too long, and milky, German skin that always burns when exposed to the sun. Mom has two major vices destructive only to her: she has an appalling diet, and cusses like a sailor. Never a drinker or smoker, I can count on one hand how many times I've seen Mom partake in any mind-altering substances.

Finally, daring to create financial freedom and ready to do what is right for her, Mom stows away enough money to replace her rotting teeth and cuts her decade plus decomposed marriage out of her life. I remember Mom relaxing on a yellow, patterned, Victorian, high back chair she reupholstered. Her sunken cheeks are a contrast to her robust but easy-going voice. The legal-size papers sit on her lap as she announces, "The divorce is final." When she speaks I can see her newborn skin emerging — black-threaded stitches in her gums with, dark, clotted blood. Cheerfully yet teen-casually, I take it in stride and congratulate her as if it was just another day in the life. At age twelve, I have other orders of business and meander out the door to hang out with my best friend.

My father finds his way in and out of our lives for some years after the divorce, but eventually he simply drifts away becoming the same wandering creature he was when I was a small child. By age 18, I have an adult understanding of the offenses my father has committed: people he has stolen from by writing bad checks, ultimately landing him in jail; the "aunts" he brought home actually being his lovers; the bruises on Mom and siblings, too frequent to be concealed as accidents; the unthinkable abuse scars left on my younger sister and horrid lies he told this frightened child to keep her from "telling;" and his unsuccessful attempts at making me yet another victim because I told on him. His addictions, his sickness, and his pain could no longer hold me hostage.

LESSONS LATER IN LIFE. One of my letting go exercises was to stop blaming my dad and mom for my own dysfunctional behavior. Revisiting history to blame others for behavior in the moment can be more a form of revenge — being angry and projecting that anger continuously to punish the culprit. The language difference is shown when "I" and "me" are used to sort out feelings: the "i" and "e" sound encourages the corners of the lips to point upward like a smile; when blaming, "you" or "you made me feel" are common words and phrases used and the lips point down like a frown.

It's tempting to assert, "but in my situation…" or "you have no idea what I've been through (therefore, I will use that to control or manipulate you)…." The truth is only you have control of who you are. It doesn't mean that an aggressor was not wrong, terrible, sick, or shouldn't be (in some cases) in prison. Reframing perceptions — cottage or castle; ugly or beautiful; evil or mentally ill; rich or poor — form peace of mind and a reality that says "I create my own perceptions of history and who I am today."

GROUP THERAPY GONE BAD

RECALL. The Adult Children of Alcoholics organization provides programs for women and men who grew up in alcoholic or other types of dysfunctional homes. Common experiences are discussed with the intention of finding freedom from the past and ways to improve lives moving forward. In my early twenties, coaxed by a friend who was aware of my background, I attended an Adult Children of Alcoholics meeting. From my perspective, this would be more accurately referred to as Adult Children of Addicts since there is rarely only one vice to overcome.

Once shuffled into the industrial tiled, dusty floored space, with stained fabric office partitions surrounding a table and chairs to give a false perception of privacy, the group exercise takes turns processing out loud. This means we share the anger, disappointment, hurt, loss, and feelings of being victimized by misdirected childhood guardians. New to this concept, this table looks like a city block with more than two dozen broken people around it. And to my utter disbelief, I am mixed in with those who repeated what they witnessed as children. Was I directed to the wrong room?

As a developing adult, I travelled in the opposite direction of my dad. I don't drink alcohol, caffeine, or even take cold and flu syrups, or pain relievers during uncomfortable menstrual cycles. My obsession is taking control of my life, getting an education, getting a good job, and making damn sure my life has absolutely no resemblance to my childhood. But, at that moment, I find myself trapped in a room of wounded souls (most either currently in a relationship with an addict or the actual addict) and I wonder, "Why the hell am I here?"

The group leader announces the process, "We'll start to my right and each person will share a memory in connection to being an adult child of an alcoholic. If you don't want to share you can say 'skip me.'" Many around the table, including me, experienced multiple tiers of dysfunction. Common to the group were emotional, physical, and/or sexual abuse. My family lived without many basics, walked on eggshells not knowing if it was going to be the "on or off the wagon" week. Those more street smart kept possessions to a minimum with lingering thoughts of being homeless, fleeing to a shelter when it became unbearable, or constantly changing residences.

Recollections pop into the tormented minds around the table. One of the people ahead in the queue began to explain, "One Christmas…" I am paralyzed. Like a whisper from an indistinguishable distance, I can hardly decipher the rest of her story. The next person in line, then the next all become white noise. Then it's my turn.

If I speak, not one word will be audible. I stare down at the faux grain surface of the table, and then wave my hand to the right to signal "skip me." The meeting is far from over.

A long-limbed man with coal black hair and dark skin, looking very much like my father, sits next to his wife and weeps as he speaks. "I have been an alcoholic and drug abuser for years and I try to stop… I want to hold down a job, have children, be a good husband and father, but I'm a terrible person that doesn't deserve…" And then, like a time bomb, I explode. Well past my turn, and dozens of agonizing stories later, I seethe with repulsion when I blurt, "You are right! You should never have children!" Two dozen heads snap in my direction. The American Indian-looking addict, who will forever battle the curse of temptation, gawks at me in shock and dismay. I shake like a startled child, and elephant-sized tears stream uncontrollably down my face, as I continue to detonate, "You ARE a terrible person! You DON'T deserve to be a father!" The chair legs make a screeching noise as I stand and shove it away from the table with the back of my legs. Every inch of my body pulsates with disgust and clearly reflects the words, "How dare you think you're the victim!" I stormed out of the make-shift conference room, past people confessing "Hi, My name is Mary and I'm…," out of support group captivity and into the sunlight, absorbing it.

LESSONS LATER IN LIFE. I never returned, and to this day have a limited interest in this type of group therapy. Preferring to be a processing loner, perhaps Proprioceptive Writing could be an effective emotional approach — light a candle, burn some incense, and listen to Baroque music while writing.

Community

RECALL. Driving through forest laden roads of Indiana I can tell we were getting closer to our destination. It's the smell of campfire. For many years our family would attend an event in Friendship, Indiana called a rendezvous for short (or formally the National Rendezvous and Living Primitive–History Foundation). We dress in a certain period of clothing; camp in a lean-to, teepee, or captain's tent; put out a trading blanket during the day and sell our merchandise to tourists and other campers; and party all night which usually includes a huge bonfire, dancing and a sundry of other activities.

Part of the custom in our household is to make our own period clothes. The summer that I became 18 years old, I spend a number of weeks making a squaw dress and leather (Indian-style) pants. It was the summer before I started college. Recently I severed a relationship with a young man who was seven years older than me because he has needs that I can't fill: living together in the country, creating dependence — buying me a car and supporting me so that I don't have to work while I attend school, marriage and children discussions.

The tasks to prepare for the upcoming event take my mind off my two year romantic connection, and interrupt any thoughts of calling him. The easiest project was the squaw dress: a loose pullover made of thin, beige, flannel-like fabric that measures directly below my knees. I cut the long sleeves at the underside of my wrist up to my armpit so that I can pull my sleeves over my shoulders when preparing food, keeping me from catching my clothes from going up in flames when working over a fire, and cleaning up around the campsite. Simple green and rust tinted ribbon was added to the dress and arm seams for a splash of color.

My cow hide pants are a bit more labor intensive. I pull apart an old pair of jeans that I no longer wear and use them as a pattern. Pinning cow hide to my jeans, I cut each piece of leather to the exact size as my former pants, dot ink where I plan to sew the pieces together, place the leather on a thick piece of wood, and punch holes in the leather by hammering the head of the ice pick into each ink mark. White noise in the background from the television, the pounding was like a rhythmic drumming. Holding the leather up to the living room window, light shining through the numerous holes was a measure of my success.

The pants are sewn together using sinew: a waxed, polyester thread that is stretch resistant (in primitive days sinew would have been made from the fibrous tissue that came from animal innards). Pushing the needle through the pelt requires a very thick thimble and needle. Sewing sessions last an hour then my fingertips scream for a break when — even when using a thimble — indentations form from gripping the needle so tightly to force it through the thick skin.

The last and most important step is getting my leather pants dirty. This becomes a rendezvous community project. No honorable buck skinner would be caught dead with a clean pair of britches so the others were obliged to wipe grease, soil, and campfire coal all over my hide — this was taken most seriously by 30+ year old men. Being young and unattached, I become the talk of the camp relatively quickly so I'm quick to demonstrate that I am not after any other woman's man by hanging out near my mother when approached by the many contributors to weathering my leather.

The morning begins with airing out the lean-to — a canvas tent with three walls and a single-pitched, sloped roof that extends all the way to the ground (so the roof is also the rear wall). Morning dew dampened blankets are collected and hung out to dry in the sun, splitting some wood and building a fire is the next order of business while someone else hauls water to fill the coffee kettle and ceramic coated pan that will be used to wash breakfast dishes and utensils.

The sound of crackling, burning wood fills the air as neighbors stumble from their tee-pees and tents with bleary eyes, muffled hair and sleep ruffled attire. Little concern for personal hygiene, with tin cups in-hand the first order of business for late risers is to scan campsites to see who has coffee kettles hanging from their tripods. If cast iron skillets sizzled with meat and eggs, those too famished to build their own fires bring their meat to throw in the same over-sized pan.

Haystacks for seats, we enjoy breakfast and conversation, wash dishes, split wood and load up the fire pit so that we can slow cook stew for our evening meal. A cast-iron pot full of beans, meat and vegetables replace the coffee kettle, and then the trading blanket is laid out.

Mom spends months preparing merchandise for the trade blanket at the rendezvous. Primarily focusing on American Indian items, she hand-crafts glass bead necklaces with special medallions, medicine bags and larger satchels for men and women. A great sense for what people are looking for at the living-history event, throughout the year she also finds little trinkets that are permitted to appear on the trade blanket — experts at the event have the right to demand items not be offered for sale if not within the historical period.

Rarely is the outside world discussed: how people spend their time outside of living history events, economic situations, world events, or the state of the current union. We cook, clean, shower, chat, eat, drink, sing, dance, play music, gather around bonfires, buy, sell and trade period merchandise together. At the close of a gathering, loose commitments of visiting one another rarely come to fruition which elevates the anticipation of meeting again — same time, same place. Watching my mom prepare for coming years (hand-crafting and buying items) reminds me of that sense of community and feeds the awareness that I want more of these types of connections year 'round.

LESSONS LATER IN LIFE. Much later in life I would come to understand the importance of support networks and how they lengthen my quality of life. The first step was acknowledging that I need people — tough for an independent, aggressive, young woman who couldn't depend on her biological family. It required that I identify people that warmed me from the inside out, who made me laugh even when I didn't want to, who I enjoyed chatting and sharing information with. It takes effort to build a community that you feel safe with, but also a willingness to give of your time, and a true interest in what others' need.

I would eventually accept that I needed my husband (which took me more than 20 years to truly embrace); realize that my innate interest in organizing professional, family and friends get-togethers was not just about serving them, but also about fueling me; and became acutely aware that some of the most interesting stories come from the most unlikely people as long as I open my ears. This is a balancing act worth the effort.

Joy of Family

In the *Sensory-Based Writing and Beginning at the End* section I talked about beginning with pictures then filling in the story. A neighbor once called my sister's family visits "the cousin love fest," and our unique take on emotional well-being springs into action when our clan, for instance, visits a restaurant (like the picture shown above).

RECALL. Like wolves, for decades we've run in a pack with our standard population being my sister's five girls, my three (two girls and one boy), my mom, my husband's brother and his wife, my husband, my sister and me (just for starters). We are a tribe that has never been capable of passing a talking stick to take turns sharing our thoughts around a fire circle so the decibels are off the charts during gatherings.

Inevitably eating establishments attempt to split up our party explaining, "We can seat you sooner." Dedicated relatives might drive six or more hours to break bread together so we respectfully decline the sit, inhale food, and leave quickly proposition.

The festivities begin in the waiting area with comments on outfits, hair, make-up, and other physical developments (from puberty, to pregnancy, to growing infants). Once multiple tables are pushed together with fifteen or more chairs squeezed around them, as if setting up at a campsite we assume control of the area. Camera flashes go off like strobe lights throughout the meal. Younger children color, play video games, and role play with dolls. A portable DVD player with multiple headphones and a stack of movies might be scattered on the food stained floor. Older teens, experimenting with goodness knows what, *tee hee hee* about their dirty little secrets with inaudible sounds that float to our end of the table — *pssssssst pssssssst pssssssst*. Occasional *Nuh Uh! Yuh Huh! Tee hee hee* snickers send shivers down our parental spines accompanied with *I really don't want to know* body language (not that they'd tell us the truth anyhow).

Inevitably servers approach our party to apologize for how long the food is taking, but we rarely notice. Before we know it hours pass.

While there is a perception of stillness when we vacate the dining room, Payton and kin energy still lingers in every corner of the establishment as chuckling, *No ways*, and a continuous ten-conversation harmony echoes until we part to our vehicles. Family ears ring as if we just left a rock concert. We dread the goodbyes. We take Facebook and family album pictures, and all bid *adieu* but always with a plan for the next time we meet.

LESSONS LATER IN LIFE. Personally, our household philosophy is kids who have parents and extended family that cultivate connection, share and make family history are happier, more optimistic, have higher self-esteem, and are sought out by their peers to absorb their positive approach to life (you know those houses where kids like to hang out, not because they get away with things but because they are nurtured). Ultimately this helps them handle adversities during childhood and beyond.

Professionally, with all the violence, disappointment and loss being endured in the world, recollecting times of love, support, and confidence is a tool that I regularly use to facilitate reframing perceptions. To self-facilitate positive feelings, one can re-experience good times by talking to family and friends about details, view photos and videos, or simply reflect using sensory detail. Finding memories and accelerating all the senses as demonstrated in many examples in this text (see, smell, touch, and hear, feel) can change your reality in an instant.

Phobias

Recall. I was elementary school age, and my sister and I shared a large bedroom with brittle, linoleum-type flooring (cold to the touch, even on a hot day). A few things stood out in my subconscious in that room: an old iron (double) bed that squeaks due to the metal frame against metal box springs; a small bookshelf by the doorway where I proudly display my piggy bank; a small vinyl record player; and a large, active beehive hanging outside the window to my left.

We don't have many toys — I have a Barbie doll and make clothes out of paper towels — so there is little reason to spend more than sleeping hours in the bedroom. The bees become progressively worse, and eventually they burrow through the wall of our bedroom turning little reason into no reason at all.

A vague vision of watching my mother with a can of bug spray lingers in my mind — the cloud of toxins, and bees swarming around her as she attempts to reclaim our space. Then my next memory is of hundreds of dead bees lying on the cold floor and tiptoeing to our bed to avoid stepping on the carcasses. I wonder, "If I step on a dead bee, does it still have a stinger?" And then I notice that some are still fidgeting: black legs and antennas searching for ways to move to an upright position with random buzzing as wings flutter futilely. Pleading to sleep elsewhere falls on my parents' deaf ears, then fear eventually wears us down to exhaustion then sleep.

There is no way of knowing how long our bedroom doubled as an insect graveyard, but my little sister (not yet in elementary school) nearly earns a tombstone. I am sitting on the steps leading upstairs playing with my Barbie in paper towel clothing when I hear my sister sobbing. I look up to see her standing on the landing between the two staircases and shout, "Mommy, Nancy looks like she's blown up a like a balloon!"

Her face all pink, eyes nearly swollen shut, cheeks full like marbles were in her mouth, face wet from tears in just panties, our mom rushes up the stairs and to the hospital. She has been stung by the bees in our room, and is deathly allergic.

Lessons later in life. Over time, I realized that I have sensitivity to bee venom as well. While not nearly as lethal as my sister, it wasn't until years later that I found out it isn't normal that you can't wear a shoe for a few days as a result of swelling from a bee sting. Over time, I would do the freak-out-when-there-is-a-bee dance complete with waving of arms and running — that turned out to be a really bad idea.

Fast forward to my 30-something years. I'm in Munich, Germany with my husband at an outdoor café. It is September, the stinging insects are very active, and I begin my dance. The waving of the arms, at first, then I made little screechy sound effects. If that wasn't enough, I stood up, still swinging my arms, moved away from my table and backed into the brace that held up the canopy over the outdoor eating area. I froze before everyone was buried by canvas. My husband and the rest of the lunching customers simply sat and stared as I lived out my perception of eminent danger. This was the very moment that I was cured of my phobia rather than enduring the death called embarrassment.

Intimidation

Recall. About 12 years old, in junior high school social studies class my girlfriend since third grade smugly yells, "We all know that you are 'Little Miss Know-It-All.'" I can't remember what the conversation revolved around, but it is about the time that I decide to study, get better grades in school and not let my friends copy my work. It is the first time I become aware of this perception. I didn't like the comment, but don't know what I want to do about it.

By the time I attend college — for my undergraduate degree — I am very strong-willed and equally as insecure. I come from a poor family and when certain wealthier peers "find me out" (see where I, and my family, live) they approach me differently (or not at all). I was relieved when I move into my own place (walking distance from the college campus). I feel like it puts me on more of an equal playing field, at least outwardly.

My reality is I am an imposter for the lion share of my undergraduate career — I have to work to maintain food, shelter, and clothing, but my education is funded through grants and scholarships (primarily because I had poor and Appalachian roots) — but I want to experience as many aspects of college life as possible which includes participating in many student organizations. As I move up the ranks in student organizations (taking executive officer positions), I adopt a habit of blatantly contradicting others. In one instance, I can't recall what I contradict, but I remember when I realize I was opposing for the sake of demonstrating my personal power.

I am standing at the front of the room with other members of an organization where I hold the position of vice president. It is more of a social gathering and someone takes a position on something, I immediately disagree and another member cheers me on. I stop, wonder why I am so irritated, realize that there is no good reason to strike down the thought (more of a habit), and announce that I jumped too quickly. At that moment I realize that I no longer want to be that person. I move away from the front of the room, I want to take a back seat, change the subject to something less political, and listen to other conversations, creating an air of agreement. I feel supportive, open, helpful, my ears and eyes feel bigger, my mouth and breathing feel relaxed. I don't feel the need to perform, to overexert my power, to compete. What possesses me to correct myself and why has such a seemingly insignificant occurrence shown up in my memory?

In the junior high and undergraduate incident I was in a place of power yet (internally) insecure. I expressed that power through answering definitively — right or wrong, black or white, giving no room for other opinions. What I realized as I matured is that definitive answers come with a price. If someone asks me for an opinion and I share an absolute thought and she follows that path then I have a responsibility for her outcome as well.

LESSONS LATER IN LIFE. Much later in life (in my late 30's) a friend was at a crossroad, shared a personal story, and asked for my opinion. I provided an answer that weighed a number of options. She responded, "You're not going to tell me what to do, are you?" It brought a smile to my face, my body was relaxed, and I was very pleased with that perception. I know many things. I don't know it all. Sweet progress.

The Intricacies of Being a Woman

Recall. I'm in elementary school, maybe third or fourth grade. In bed, fast asleep, I'm awakened by women and girls screaming, and the echoing of hands smacking skin. "Git off a me!" screeches a young woman. I leap out of my bed, slowly open my bedroom window that faces the street and peer out with the light off. Multiple generations of women-folk — 7 to 70 years old — have arms flailing then my 20-something, neighbor's long locks are wadded in an intruder's hand. Bent at the waist, face down, looking at the sidewalk, her grandma moves into the middle of the chaos as if her age is armor. If I were being polite I would say she was petite but she is more emaciated, cancer-like; with unnaturally colored dark hair; denture-less sunken cheeks; a house dress that snaps in the front; stockings that she rolls up to her knees; with slip-on, house shoes; and a cigarette resting between her nicotine-stained index and middle fingers. As she bellows out curse words with her raspy voice, her body goes into automatic remembering how she whipped her kids into shape when she was a young mother not expecting to be hit back.

The elderly woman's presumption works, her daughter's hair is set free, and the scuttle concludes with a shouting match accompanied with future threats. Bearing witness, hugging the threshold of the door is the granddaughter. A few years younger than I, as I observe from above she stands in the bowels of deprived judgment hell. Being cautious not to draw attention two stories up, I carefully close the drape and return safely to my bed.

I figure out (for the most part) how to walk on egg shells in my home with my dad. Becoming street smart is the next life lesson. It is most common for those who live in my area not to hold down a regular job. Common income streams include: welfare, long-term worker's compensation, drugs, robbing trains, and stealing wire and other items out of condemned homes.

I do my best not to overhear conversations about illegal activity or who is going to kick whose butt so I won't be dragged into a support group or mob. I am too petite to be considered tough with the masses, but driven by fear that things can go bad at any second, I protect myself by understanding how others interpret being respected. For instance, when the grandma places her lawn chair on the sidewalk in front of her house and gazes at cars rolling by while smoking a cigarette I might say, "Hi, Mrs. 'X'" and continue walking (almost like earning a pass). If she asks any questions in return, a sound strategy is to answer politely with few words and vacate the area quickly to avoid more family joining her.

If her daughter joins her I can expect an insult. My response includes very little eye contact (similar to a puppy responding to an alpha mama dog), a polite laugh, and a quick excuse to evacuate. The majority of the time I can wiggle out of conversations and altercations, but the older I become the more time others demand, especially as I get taller.

There is an element of safety that comes from being flat-chested with no girly curves. The worse thing that can happen is I am the brunt of others' jokes (I can laugh along then make a quick exit). Boobs are like lively flags waving on young women's chests, and if displayed too proudly competition develops. Luckily, while in this neighborhood, I'm physically behind all my girlfriends: very slender, and brassieres are wannabe accessories.

Initially the attention that came from transitioning from playing with Barbie's to becoming the Barbie was exciting, but when pheromones enter the equation it's an entirely new learning experience. My orientation begins when working a minimum wage job while in college. My 20-something manager needs a ride home from work. Of course, I am happy to oblige but when I come to work the next day I am physically threatened by his young wife. My manager says nothing to remedy the situation — I am completely perplexed.

Once earning my undergraduate degree and entering the professional workforce in my early 20's, I sense discomfort from executives' wives, and a self-elected coach, 60-something, male workmate advises me at a company party, "don't laugh as much." Okay. That's like telling me not to breath.

An equation is emerging: boobs plus laugh equals bad. Adding to the complexity, at another work function my uterus enters the mix when the president of the same international company announces during a meal with 8 other workmates (including my manager and manager's manager who are both women), "I'm sure you'll just get pregnant and leave" (similar to the young woman I replaced). I quit, but not because I was with child.

But wait, there's more! A 70-something, advertising agency president feels comfortable enough to philosophize in front of me and the highest ranking executives of another international company that signs my paychecks (when I am seven months pregnant), "I don't blame you for not staying home with your children. I blame men." When I become friendly with wives of male workmates, there still seems to be a cloud lingering over our relationships. Once I kidded with a workmate's wife, "Oh, you know how your husband can be." She retorts, "No. Why don't you tell me about my husband?!"

Only a few more years would pass when I finally decide that corporate America was not the best environment for me. The vice president of an independently-owned company that I moved to — claiming to be state of the art and was eventually sold to a large packaged goods company —

declares only two months into my employment at a sales meeting, "You won't last. You'll just get pregnant and leave."

LESSONS LATER IN LIFE. Competitive environments are equivalent to my childhood fight or flight surroundings: combative and designed to bring some people up and others down. To survive those settings people must have protective shields, determine how to ride through the rough patches, and exit situations as gracefully as possible. The best route for me is if I experience discomfort due to a perception that thriving is limited I look inward, at myself, to re-anchor more positive thinking. I'm not saying that challenges still don't arise, but I can think more clearly and make better decisions. Ultimately, in my 40's I transitioned into more relaxing work, people and environments that authentically embrace more harmonious interactions.

BREAKING ABUSIVE PATTERNS

RECALL. It's my senior year in high school. My father is beginning to spread his wings: he found another unsuspecting woman to latch onto, marry and abuse. By this time my mom and dad have been divorced about five years, but in our family's continuous odd form he has a bedroom upstairs and my mom sleeps on the couch downstairs. Dad is drinking less right now so he works and contributes money to the household.

He brings his new lady friend to the house like he had when he was still married to my mother, but this time we didn't have to make-believe she was our Aunt and put up with the chaos that surrounded his affairs. She is younger than he: 15 or so years his junior, unnaturally dyed black hair that puddles a few inches past her shoulders, wears blue jeans and faux leather, medium heeled go-go-dancer looking boots that hug her legs. Putting on a gallant stage act, my father asks if I approve of them being married and I respond as I move toward the closest exit, "Whatever makes you happy, dad." This amuses both of them and allows me to slip quickly out the door.

Even with his new found partner, we aren't totally rid of his drinking binges. One night when Cutty Sark whisky — his drink of choice — lingered in the air I quietly pad up the stairs and tiptoe past his room to enter my own. This promises to be even more difficult because I have to silently unlock the padlock on my door (which is an even longer story). Unfortunately, dad hasn't passed out yet, sees me and begins to slur inquiries. I don't remember the subject, but I do remember our voices elevating and his arm extending to hit me. His success is marked by blacking my eye.

Going to school the next day, I don't think anyone will notice, but many inquire about my "injury" and I spout off the dumbest thing ever, "I ran into a door." I couldn't change the story because that would raise suspicion, so when I stumble through my excuse in homeroom I remember looking out of the corner of my eye noticing my teacher squint and purse his lips nonverbally expressing, "Sure you did."

After a long day of excuses I am relieved to get home. Bruises on the butt and even the arms can be hidden, but embarrassment amongst my peers is like wearing a badge of shame. I don't speak to my father, nor do I accept attempted apologies like he had given to my mother for so many years: "I didn't mean to… You know better than to make me angry.…" So he writes me a note.

He slides the message on a piece of tattered paper, written in light pencil under my bedroom door. Astonished, it is the first time I realize that my father can't spell, use punctuation or put a cohesive sentence together to express his complete thoughts. Masking this with fine penmanship would not have made much difference.

A small, yet significant, example while writing this passage is when my son got up late for school (a third year, university, undergraduate). I make him coffee, toast and a protein before he runs out the door, but he is throwing a tantrum that includes not having cream in his coffee. My husband reflects, "What if you were his wife and insecure and he spoke to you that way? What if he ranted like this if he had children?" I replied, "He will feel guilty today, just like my dad," and sure enough I find a note on my home office desk that day, "I'm sorry about this morning. You help me in so many ways that I couldn't do it without you. I love you mom." Contrasts drift to mind — the writing of my educated son and that of my fathers — but has the chain been broken?

LESSONS LATER IN LIFE.

When I was a younger mother (20 and 30-something) yelling was a frequent habit. Over time and lots of inner work I realized that it wasn't worth damaging valuable brain cells to stress myself and others out. My dad didn't have the fortitude or resources to express or move past his anger effectively. With patience and mindfulness we are all breaking the chain.

Conclusion

NO EXCUSES! GET TO WRITING!

There's really no excuse not to record your thoughts (at least privately). I remember a gal in her 80's who attended one of my independent writing workshops who said, "I hate writing," and yet she occupied a seat for three hours that day! What she was really saying is that she didn't feel confident putting words to paper; however, when she talked about her handmade product line she couldn't be stopped. The solution: audio record all of her thoughts, transcribe, do some silent writing to fill in some gaps, then intuitively punctuate and — voila — you've got a great document!

Sure, there are style sheets and rules that need to be followed when publishing in a variety of situations, but it's important to break the habit that says writing is only a silent, formal activity. Most carry a cellular phone with a recording device to transcribe thoughts, and all have access to a writing or typing utensil and recording surface (paper or computer). Heck, now there is even voice-activated word processing. You've already got what it takes — your natural voice.

Creative writers, journaling followers and the measurable minded now understand how storytelling aloud, writing and even reading experiences are enhanced through this process. Put your reimaginable personal experiences (including science observations), and material you have personal connections to on paper or other mediums now. Release perfection shackles — the need to write an extensive, mechanical, introduction before you even know what you're going to fluidly write about, staring at that comma or sentence (in rough draft phase) because it doesn't flow quite right, believing that you can silent write the perfect document in a first draft so you skip extra content building steps, creating a standardized format upfront that ties your creative hands.

Carve out a customized path that plays to your individual strengths to fully express your thoughts. Past training or schooling may keep you from embracing certain concepts that I've shared, but if you've gotten this far in the book (the conclusion, nonetheless) build your own bridges referencing the published papers and books as well as the pieces of the sensory-based writing process that you resonate with. This is not a traditional banking approach depositing hard and fast rules into your head, but the process can enhance everything you have learned and retained on how to get from writing point "a" to writing point "b."

Now, it's time marry your natural voice and the sensory realm with material where you are fluid, expert, and confident. You can revise and polish to play by others' rules later, but at the end of the day you can't edit if there is nothing on paper. Get to it!

References

Bhullar, N., Schutte, N.S., & Malouff, J.M. (2011). Writing about satisfaction processes increases well-being. *Individual Differences Research, 9(1)*, 22-32. Retrieved from www.idr-journal.com

Dawkins, J. (2003). Teaching meaning-based punctuation. *Teaching English in the Two-Year College, 31(2)*, 154-162. Retrieved from http://www.ncte.org/journals/tetyc/issues/v31-2. Copyright 2003 by the National Council of Teachers of English. Used with permission.

Dolores, P., Keselman, & A., Monopoli. M. (2003). The academic writing of community college remedial students: Text and learner variables. *Higher Education, 45(1)*, 19-42. Retrieved fromhttp://www.sitemaker.umich.edu/gsco/files/perinetal_highered_2003.pdf

Elbow, P. (2012). *Vernacular eloquence: What speech can bring to writing.* New York, NY: Oxford University Press.

Fillmer, H. T. & Parkay, F.W. (1985). How can hypnosis improve reading proficiency?, *The Clearing House, 59(2)*, 61-63. doi: 10.1080/00098655.1985.9955605

Frattaroli, J., Thomas, M., & Lyubomirsky, S. (2011). Opening up in the classroom: Effects ofexpressive writing on graduate school entrance exam performance, *Emotion, 11(3)*, 691-696. doi: 10.1037/a0022946

Frey, H. (1980). Improving the performance of poor readers through autogenic relaxation training. *The Reading Teacher, 33(8)*, 928-932. Retrieved from http://www.jstor.org/stable/20195149 (usage approved by Wiley Publications, www.wiley.com).

Gee, J.P. (2007), What video games have to teach us about learning literacy. New York, NY: Palgrave Macmillan.

Holland, R. (2013). Writing experiences of community college students with self-reported writing anxieties and linguistic insecurity: A perspective for college counselors, *Community College Journal of Research and Practice, 37(4)*, 278-295. doi:10.1080/10668920903527084

Lenhart, A., Arafeh, S., Smith, A., & Macgill, A. (2008).What teens tell us encourages them to write. *Pew Research Center*. Retrieved from http://www.pewinternet.org/2008/04/24/what-teens-tell-us-encourages-them-to-write/

Marinelli, R., Bindi, R., Marchi, S., Castellani, E., Carli, G., & Santarcangelo, E. L. (2012). Hypnotizability-related differences in written language. *Intl. Journal of Clinical and Experimental Hypnosis, 60(1)*, 54–66. doi: 10.1080/00207144.2011.622196

Martinez, C. T., Kock, N., & Cass, J. (2011). Pain and pleasure in short essay writing: Factors predicting university students' writing anxiety and writing self-efficacy. *Journal of Adolescent & Adult Literacy, 54(5)*, 351-360. doi: 10.1598

Meena, B., & Wallace, A. (2013). Writing-to-learn,Writing-to-communicate, & scientific literacy. *The American Biology Teacher, 75(3)*, 170-175. doi: http://dx.doi.org/10.1525/abt.2013.75.3.5

Metcalf, L.T. & Simon, T. (2002). Writing the mind alive: The proprioceptive method for finding authentic voice. New York, NY: The Ballantine Publishing Group.

Moffet, J. (1983). Reading and writing as meditation. *Language Arts, 60(3)*, 315-322. Retrieved from http://www.jstor.org/stable/41962389. Copyright 1983 by the National Council of Teachers of English. Used with permission.

Schultz, J. (1977) The story workshop method: Writing from start to finish. *College English, 39(4)*. 411-436. doi: 10.2307/375765. Copyright 1977 by the National Council of Teachers of English. Used with permission.

Slatcher, R.B. & Pennebaker, J.W. (2006). How do I love thee? Let me count the words: the social effects of expressive writing. *Sage Publications, 17(8)*, 660-664. Copyright 2006 by the Association of Psychological Science. Reprinted (summarized only) by Permission of SAGE Publications. doi:10.1111/j.1467-9280.2006.01762.x

Stanton, H.E. (1986). Writing Block? Try Self-Hypnosis. *College Teaching, 34(2)*. 75-79. doi: 10.1080/87567555.1986.9926772

About The Author

Michelle developed a sense of how to read situations quickly in order to survive a childhood household of anger, poverty, alcohol, drug, mental and physical abuse, and parents divorcing at an early age. As an adult, in order to manifest positive outcomes in her own life, Michelle became fascinated with how people problem solve and how their minds' work. Her eclectic (mainstream and conscious living) studies over the past 25+ years evolved to sharing tools to become more comfortable individually and with others. She (personally) moved past limiting history and physical conditions to a marriage/partnership of over 30 years, three bright kids (yes, there have been challenges), and a joyful, healthy life.

All Michelle's professional training plays a part in her work to co-facilitate building self-confidence, achieving individual voice, and creating effective collaborations professionally and personally. Michelle's **mind over matter solutions specialties** are Hypnosis — Doctor of Clinical Hypnotherapy; Self-Hypnosis; EFT (Emotional Freedom Technique); NLP (Neuro-Linguistic Programming); Acupressure Hypnosis (creating Emotional Balancing Points); Past Life Regression; Sensory-Based Writing and Coaching that also pulls from her graduate (**academic**) studies in English (Rhetoric, Composition, and Professional Writing), Undergraduate degree in Communication Arts, skills that result from numerous years of French independent studies, and experiences writing eight self-help books; and independent studies to assess personalities using Astrology, Numerology, and Birth Order to more quickly tap into individual needs. In addition, writing and connecting to others' needs (individually, the masses, and in business) is a part of her mainstream work and includes being an adjunct college English instructor, and accomplished national brand marketing manager with extensive national and international advertising, marketing, research, writing, speaking and business building experience.

More information on Michelle's background, books, events, community collaborations, teaching, and her private practice can be found at www.MichellePayton.com, www.MichellePaytonWriter.com, www.TheLeftSide.com, or by doing a simple internet search on "Michelle Payton."

She, her husband and life partner since 1982, and two of three children live, work and play in Asheville, North Carolina.

Conscious Living & Self-Help Books with Michelle A. (M.A.) Payton

As a conscious living and mind over matter solutions professional, Michelle's work focuses on how to accomplish 21st century, soul-based living as a mainstream and conscious parent, partner, professional, and individual, including how this has unfolded for her, her clients and throughout history.

Adventures of a Mainstream Metaphysical Mom: Choosing Peace of Mind in a World of Diverse Ideas (Book 1)

Mainstream metaphysical parenting, mentoring, and relationships with self and others in the 21st century!

2003 Finalist for Best Biographical/Self-Help Book
—Coalition of Visionary Resources, 2003 Visionary Awards, International New Age Trade Show
192 pp ~ paperback
ISBN 978-0-9719804-0-2
$13.95

"Soul"utions: Achieving Financial, Intellectual, Physical, Social, and Spiritual Balance with Soul

Thoughts on soul-based living using goal setting principles in all areas of life!

239 pp ~ paperback
ISBN 978-0-9719804-1-9
$14.95

Birth Mix Patterns™: Astrology, Numerology, and Birth Order, and their Effects on the Past, Present, and Future

Analyzes hundreds of historical figures, including United States Presidents and First Ladies, artists, authors, civil rights leaders, and more in connection with astrology, numerology, and birth order.

2006 Finalist for Best General Interest/How To Book
—Coalition of Visionary Resources, 2006 Visionary Awards, International New Age Trade Show

160 pp ~ paperback
ISBN 978-0-9719804-2-6
$12.95

Conscious Living & Self-Help Books with Michelle A. (M.A.) Payton

Birth Mix Patterns™: Astrology, Numerology, and Birth Order, and their Effects on the Families & Other Groups that Matter

Analyzes the authors of the Declaration of Independence, dark leaders, the US Supreme Court Justices, the Beatles and more in connection with astrology, numerology, and birth order.

133 pp ~ paperback
ISBN 978-0-9719804-3-3
$12.95

Birth Mix Patterns™ and Loving Relationships using Astrology, Numerology, and Birth Order

Analyzes more than two dozen famous couples from Hollywood, to community servers, to same gender partnerships in connection with astrology, numerology, and birth order.

137 pp ~ paperback
ISBN 978-0-9719804-4-0
$12.95

Healing What's Real: Expanding Your Personal Power with Mind Over Matter Techniques

Dr. Payton shares her experiences with Hypnotherapy, Neuro-Linguistic Programming™ (NLP), Emotional Freedom Technique™ (EFT), meditation, and more with dozens of transcribed sessions and interviews combining these techniques.

253 pp ~ paperback
ISBN 978-0-9719804-5-7
$15.95

More Adventures of a Mainstream Metaphysical Mom: Finding Peace While Raising Teens, Building a Community, and Consciously Following-Through (Book 2)

More on mainstream metaphysical parenting, mentoring, and relationships as she and her family ages and wades through constant changes and few hard and fast rules.

225 pp ~ paperback
ISBN 978-0-9719804-6-4
$12.95

Index

A

Adventures of a Mainstream Metaphysical Mom 2, 3, 18, 67, 79
adversity 63, 76, 88
authentic voice 32

B

Beauty and the Beast 64
Brainstorming Process 67

C

calm university students 34, 54
Columbia University 34
courage to write 16

D

Darwin, Charles 40
David Copperfield 16
Dawkins, John 22, 32, 40
Diary of Anne Frank 40
Dickens, Charles 16
disabled readers
  coached imagery 35

E

EFT™. *See* Emotional Freedom Technique™

Elbow, Peter 24, 25, 32, 39, 40, 53
Emotional Freedom Technique 124
expressive writing 36–37, 39, 53, 59
  enhanced performance 38
  raises scores 36

F

Feynman, Richard 40
Frank, Anne 40

G

grammar 5, 20, 21, 22, 24

H

hypnosis 12, 37, 38, 120
hypnotherapy
  creates more writing content 32

I

imagery 38–39
improve performance 35

J

journaling 41

L

laboratory work 49
learner 20, 43
   audio 43, 44
   tactile 43, 45
   visual 43
LSAT 36

M

MCAT 36
meaning-based punctuation 22
meditation 39

N

National Association of Biology Teachers 36
natural pause grammar 22, 24
natural voice 11, 12, 13, 19, 20, 22, 28, 33, 40, 44, 60, 75, 76, 117, 118
natural written voice 18, 28
Neuro-Linguistic Programming 12, 43
NLP™. *See* Neuro-Linguistic Programming™
normal speech in writing 39

O

oral pause 25
ordinary language 32
ordinary writing 59

P

PhD academic output 37
polish 66
Pride & Prejudice 64
problem solving 71
proprioceptive method 41
proprioceptive writing 100
punctuation 5, 20, 21, 23, 24, 28, 29

R

reading improves writing 38–39
reading to write and speak 75
reduce apprehension 34
reframe grammar and punctuation 32
rubric
   academic 26
   customized 27
   democracy 27
   standard 27
Russell, Bertrand 40

S

science based 49
science exploration 31, 36
self-facilitate 28
self-hypnosis 37
selfie 15, 16, 63
self-portrait 16
self-portrait writing 46
self-reflection 36–37
sensory-based writing 11, 28–31, 59, 60, 76, 104
sensory experiences 46
sensory writing and science 49
silent writing 20, 28
sliding scale punctuation 22, 23, 24, 28, 29
sliding value punctuation 22
Snow White 64
Stanton, Harry 32, 38
StoryShare 28
story workshop 37

T

teens write 33
test anxiety 53
therapeutic environments 41

V

Vernacular Eloquence 25, 39, 53
video games 35
visualization 55

W

writer's block 19, 20, 38, 68

www.ingramcontent.com/pod-product-compliance
Lightning Source LLC
LaVergne TN
LVHW051645080426
835511LV00016B/2502